PRAISE FOR *MOON SIGNS, HOUSES & HEALING*

"Carmen Turner-Schott has written a wonderful astrology book about the moon's magical way of filling us with empowering energy, self-healing, and creative passion. She describes in great depth the self-caring and transformative power offered to us by our own moon sign. When I read the description of my Aries moon, I was amazed how Carmen tuned into my emotional nature and what I needed to focus on in my life to stay emotionally centered. This book is a must read whether you are new to astrology or a seasoned professional like myself. I love the message embedded throughout this book: being true to the intuitive nature of the moon leads us to walk along uplifting paths to happiness and creative enjoyment!"

—Bernie Ashman, author of *Sun Signs and Past Lives*

T0008531

MOON SIGNS
HOUSES
& HEALING

ABOUT THE AUTHOR

Carmen Turner-Schott, MSW, LISW, is a practicing clinical social worker, author, and psychological astrologer with national and international clientele. She graduated from Washington University in St. Louis with a Master of Social Work degree in 1999. She has worked with victims of trauma for over twenty-five years.

Carmen began her astrological work at the age of sixteen, after an experience with a glowing ball of light in her doorway. She began studying religion, astrology, and metaphysics at that time. She has lectured and presented astrology workshops and eGroups for the Association of Research and Enlightenment (A.R.E). She also enjoys teaching a variety of spiritual development classes.

Carmen has been researching astrology, transformation, and healing. She founded the Astrological Self Awareness Center in 2005 and later changed the name to Deep Soul Divers Astrology. She has a passion for researching astrology and specializes in the eighth and twelfth astrological houses and their effects on trauma, healing, and resiliency. Her most recent books are *Sun Signs, Houses & Healing: Build Resilience and Transform Your Life through Astrology* and *The Mysteries of the Twelfth Astrological House: Fallen Angels*. Both can be purchased on Amazon.

You can learn more about Carmen at www.carmenturnerschott.com; on her Facebook author page, www.facebook.com/CarmenTurnerSchottWriter; and on her professional site, www.facebook.com/deepsouldiversastrology.com.

CARMEN
TURNER-SCHOTT

MOON SIGNS
HOUSES
& HEALING

GAIN EMOTIONAL
STRENGTH & RESILIENCE
THROUGH
ASTROLOGY

Llewellyn Publications
Woodbury, Minnesota

First Edition
First Printing, 2023

Cover design by Cassie Willett
Chart illustration on page 13 from Astro Dienst, www.astro.com
Interior art by Llewellyn Art Department

Llewellyn Publications is a registered trademark of Llewellyn Worldwide Ltd.

Library of Congress Cataloging-in-Publication Data (Pending)
ISBN: 978-0-7387-7396-4

Llewellyn Worldwide Ltd. does not participate in, endorse, or have any authority or responsibility concerning private business transactions between our authors and the public.

All mail addressed to the author is forwarded but the publisher cannot, unless specifically instructed by the author, give out an address or phone number.

Any internet references contained in this work are current at publication time, but the publisher cannot guarantee that a specific location will continue to be maintained. Please refer to the publisher's website for links to authors' websites and other sources.

Llewellyn Publications
A Division of Llewellyn Worldwide Ltd.
2143 Wooddale Drive
Woodbury, MN 55125-2989
www.llewellyn.com

Printed in the United States of America

To my daughter, Bella. Always remember the positive things about having your moon in Capricorn.

♈ ♉ ♊ ♋ ♌ ♍

CONTENTS

Introduction

Everyone can benefit from understanding what makes them feel happy, passionate, and emotionally fulfilled. The moon sign in astrology reveals a person's unconscious motives and deeper emotions. In this book we are going to discuss how each moon sign heals, transforms, and becomes more resilient. The moon sign has a powerful influence on every area of your life. Let's begin by talking about the importance of self-care.

WHAT IS SELF-CARE?

Most of us don't make adequate time to take care of ourselves. Recently, I had the opportunity to ask several leaders in my community what they do for self-care. They admitted that they don't do a good job of taking care of their own stress or emotional needs; many sacrificed personal issues for their career goals. They said self-care was something that was challenging for them to implement in their daily lives. I realized that implementing self-care is something that we all struggle with.

I have worked in the helping profession for many years and have witnessed this issue on a daily basis. Most of us are more comfortable helping others than ourselves. We sacrifice our own energy, emotions, and time for other people. We put our emotional needs on the back burner and neglect ourselves. It's important that we learn how to nurture our own needs.

Self-care involves a deliberate effort to make time for reflection, relaxation, grounding, and doing activities that help us let go of stressful emotions. It needs to become part of our daily routine. It helps us understand what is truly important in our lives. Examples of self-care are taking breaks, healthy eating, exercising, asking for help, spending time alone, putting yourself first, setting boundaries, forgiving yourself, and participating in your hobbies. One reason self-care techniques do not work the same for everyone is because of the unique way our moon sign (and the house the moon is in) affects our ability to react to stress, heal, relax, and recharge.

Self-care tips work differently for each moon sign. Those with moon signs with compatible elements, like water/earth and fire/air, will benefit from similar activities. Gaining a deeper understanding of your emotional nature and what makes you happy is an important part of self-care. This book will help you on your self-care journey.

WHAT IS A BIRTH CHART?

Astrology is a powerful tool that can be used to understand your emotional nature. The moon sign is one of the most important placements in astrology. The moon represents your inner nature. By studying astrology, you can learn to interpret birth charts, including your own. You will be able to determine what sign and house the moon is in. This will help you gain a deeper understanding about the emotional nature of yourself and others.

Everyone has a birth chart. It is an image of the astrological and planetary placements at your exact moment of birth. Your birth chart reveals your emotional nature, basic personality traits, how you think, how you love, what type of careers you are drawn to, intuitive abilities, creative talents, childhood experiences, personal relationships, and this lifetime's soul mission.

In this book, we are focusing on moon signs and house placements. Learning more about your moon sign will help validate things you already know about yourself. And by studying your birth chart's moon and house placement, you can learn more about your deeper needs.

WHAT ARE THE ZODIAC SIGNS?

There are twelve moon signs in astrology. Each moon sign is ruled by a certain natural element. The four elements exist in nature and are fire, air, earth, and water. Each sign is categorized by a certain modality: cardinal, fixed, or mutable. The modality that rules your moon sign has a significant impact on your emotional nature; it reveals a deeper part of your personality that others might not see.

Each moon sign is associated with a planet, and the energy of that planet influences your moon sign personality. For example, Aries is ruled by Mars and is full of energy and passion. Mercury, the planet of communication and thinking, is associated with both Virgo and Gemini. Libra and Taurus are both influenced by Venus, the planet of love, harmony, and relationships.

The fire signs are full of energy and drive; they are Aries, Leo, and Sagittarius. Earth signs are practical, reliable, and cautious; they are Taurus, Virgo, and Capricorn. The air signs are intellectual, freedom loving, and emotionally detached; they are Gemini,

Libra, and Aquarius. Water signs are emotional, creative, and imaginative; they are Cancer, Scorpio, and Pisces.

Every moon sign has an opposite emotional nature, and that is represented by its polar opposite sign. Every sign's polar opposite shares the same modality (cardinal, fixed, or mutable). The polar opposite signs are also highly compatible because they share a compatible element (earth/water or fire/air). For instance, Virgo is a mutable earth sign. The polar opposite of a Virgo moon is a Pisces moon, which is a mutable water sign. Virgo moons are practical, perfectionistic, and detail oriented, while their opposite—Pisces moons—are imaginative, creative, and compassionate. The interesting thing about your polar-opposite moon sign is that you often attract them into your life. They will be able to touch your heart and make you feel comfortable. In relationships, you're most compatible with them because they share similar emotional reactions and help balance you out. They are the yin to your yang, so to speak.

Below is an easy reference guide that has each moon sign and its element, symbol, planetary ruler, polar opposite, and modality.

Sign	Element	Modality	Planetary Ruler	Polar Opposite Sign	Symbol
Aries	Fire	Cardinal	Mars	Libra	The ram
Taurus	Earth	Fixed	Venus	Scorpio	The bull
Gemini	Air	Mutable	Mercury	Sagittarius	The twins
Cancer	Water	Cardinal	Moon	Capricorn	The crab
Leo	Fire	Fixed	Sun	Aquarius	The lion

Sign	Element	Modality	Planetary Ruler	Polar Opposite Sign	Symbol
Virgo	Earth	Mutable	Mercury	Pisces	The maiden
Libra	Air	Cardinal	Venus	Aries	The scales
Scorpio	Water	Fixed	Pluto	Taurus	The scorpion
Sagittarius	Fire	Mutable	Jupiter	Gemini	The archer
Capricorn	Earth	Cardinal	Saturn	Cancer	The goat
Aquarius	Air	Fixed	Uranus	Leo	The water bearer
Pisces	Water	Mutable	Neptune	Virgo	The fish

Moon signs have special symbols or glyphs associated with them, just like sun signs. Aries starts the zodiac as the first sign; it's ruled by the planet Mars and is known as the Ram. The second sign is Taurus the Bull and is ruled by the planet Venus. The third sign, Gemini, is ruled by Mercury and is known as the Twins. Cancer is the fourth sign, ruled by the moon, and its symbol is the crab. Leo the Lion is the fifth sign and is ruled by the sun. The sixth sign is Virgo the Maiden, and it is ruled by the planet Mercury. The seventh sign is Libra, ruled by Venus and represented as the scales of balance. Scorpio is the eighth sign; its symbol is the scorpion and it is associated with Pluto. The ninth sign is Sagittarius the Archer, ruled by the planet Jupiter. Capricorn the Goat is the tenth sign and is ruled by Saturn. Aquarius is the eleventh sign, known as the Water Bearer, and is ruled by the planet Uranus. The last sign of the zodiac is Pisces the Fish, ruled by Neptune.

Each of the twelve moon signs are represented by images called *glyphs*. The glyphs often represent the symbols associated with each zodiac sign. For example, Taurus is the Bull, and its glyph looks similar to a bull with horns. In the following chart, you can find the symbol for each moon sign.

Moon Sign Glyph	Moon Sign	Moon Sign Glyph	Moon Sign
♈	Aries	♎	Libra
♉	Taurus	♏	Scorpio
♊	Gemini	♐	Sagittarius
♋	Cancer	♑	Capricorn
♌	Leo	♒	Aquarius
♍	Virgo	♓	Pisces

WHAT ARE THE PLANETS?

The planets in a birth chart are also symbolized by glyphs. You will need to know the symbol of the moon in order to find it on the birth chart wheel. For the purposes of this book, we will be working with the moon's planetary placement, denoted by a crescent-shaped symbol.

Each moon sign has a planetary ruler. Each planet has a certain energy that impacts the moon sign's personality and influences our emotional nature. The ten planets in astrology are the sun, moon, Mercury, Venus, Mars, Jupiter, Saturn, Uranus, Neptune, and Pluto. Four signs share the same ruling planets:

- The sun rules Leo.

- The moon rules Cancer.

- Mercury rules Virgo and Gemini.

- Venus rules Libra and Taurus.

- Mars rules Aries.

- Jupiter rules Sagittarius.

- Saturn rules Capricorn.

- Uranus rules Aquarius.

- Neptune rules Pisces.

- Pluto rules Scorpio.

When two moon signs share a planetary ruler, such as Libra and Taurus, they are attracted to each other. Both Libra and Taurus moons are ruled by Venus. They crave peace, harmony, and comfort. Both signs dislike conflict and being rushed to make decisions. Even though they are two different elements (air and earth), they complement each other and share a similar emotional nature.

Glyph	Planet	Description
☉	Sun	Rules the sign Leo. The sun represents our main identity, personality, and ego. Symbolically, it also represents the father figure in a birth chart. The house where the sun is placed is where we like to shine.
☽	Moon	Rules the sign Cancer. The moon represents our emotional nature and inner life. The moon also represents the mother figure. How we express our feelings depends on which house and sign the moon is in.
☿	Mer-cury	Rules the signs Virgo and Gemini. Mercury represents thoughts, ideas, and the way we communicate. Wherever Mercury is placed is where we express ourself best, both through writing and speaking.
♀	Venus	Rules the signs Taurus and Libra. Venus represents our loving nature and values. Venus symbolizes the way we express our love and feelings. Wherever Venus is placed is where we experience and seek harmony.
♂	Mars	Rules the sign Aries. Mars represents our drive, energy, aggression, and impulses. Wherever Mars is placed is where we strive to succeed; it shows what we are very competitive about. It can also show where we experience conflict in life.
♃	Jupiter	Rules the sign Sagittarius. Jupiter represents expansion, abundance, education, and travel. Jupiter shows where we benefit and experience good luck and fortune.

Glyph	Planet	Description
♄	Saturn	Rules the sign Capricorn. Saturn represents where we feel discipline and responsibility, as well as where we feel restricted. Wherever Saturn is placed in a birth chart is where we feel uncomfortable and limited. We must work hard to overcome this restricting energy.
♅	Uranus	Rules the sign Aquarius. Uranus represents our individuality and uniqueness. Anything unorthodox is Uranus energy. Uranus can represent sudden changes and the unexpected.
♆	Neptune	Rules the sign Pisces. Neptune represents spirituality, illusions, drugs, and music. Neptune shows where we find spirituality, where we can delude ourselves, and where we are idealistic. It is associated with addiction, such as alcoholism or anything that helps us escape reality.
♇	Pluto	Rules the sign Scorpio. Pluto represents transformation and regeneration. Pluto is where we experience powerful spiritual and psychological changes within ourselves and the environment. Pluto is intense energy that is associated with sex, death, and other people's resources.

WHAT ARE THE HOUSES?

In this book you will be able to look up what house in your birth chart the moon is located in. An in-depth explanation of the moon in each house will be discussed in chapter 13.

The twelve houses in a birth chart represent significant areas of life. The houses are represented by sections of the sky. In the middle of the astrological wheel is the earth. Imagine standing inside that wheel and looking up at the sky. The sky is then divided into twelve sections, which are what astrologers call *houses*.

- **The first house** starts the birth chart wheel and represents our main personality, appearance, and identity. It is known as the *ascendant* or *rising sign,* and it creates the first impression we make in the world because it affects how others perceive us. The first house relates to how we handle stress.

- **The second house** is the house of money, finances, and self-worth. It's where we find comfort, security, and stability.

- **The third house** represents communication, siblings, and basic learning. It can also represent short journeys, publishing, radio, and television.

- **The fourth house** is the house of home and family. It is associated with the moon and the mother. It is known as the *Imum Coeli* and sits at the bottom of the birth chart wheel.

- **The fifth house** is the house of children, creativity, and fun. It represents love affairs, pleasure, and gambling.

- **The sixth house** is the house of work, routine, and health. This is the house of service, coworkers, and daily life.

- **The seventh house** is known as the *descendant* and rules marriage and partnership.

- **The eighth house** is the house of death, transformation, healing, rebirth, trauma, and deep experiences.

- **The ninth house** is the house of travel, foreigners, higher education, and religion.

- **The tenth house** is the career house. It is known as the *midheaven* because it sits at the top of the birth chart wheel. This is the house of success, achievement, and the public.

- **The eleventh house** represents friendship, groups, and humanitarian causes.

- **The twelfth house** is the house of sacrifice, spirituality, escapism, and service to others. This house represents the unconscious and subconscious mind. It relates to sleep, dreams, and altered states of consciousness.

The emotional energy of your moon sign is expressed in one of these areas of life.

In the coming chapters, I will describe people based on which sign or house their moon is in. For example, I might call people with the moon in Aries "Aries moon people," "Aries moons," or "first house people," which is simply how I describe people with that placement.

CALCULATING YOUR MOON SIGN

The moon sign can be calculated by determining three things: date of birth, place of birth, and exact time of birth. The amazing thing about the moon is that it moves quickly through the twelve astrological signs; it stays in each sign for approximately a two-day period. Depending on the location of your birth, it might stay in one sign for the entire day. It moves through every sign within a month. Because of this, you will need an accurate birth time to calculate your moon sign placement. If you are not sure of the exact time of birth, you can still get an approximate calculation if you know the time of day you were born; see what sign and house the moon is in for that rough period of time.

I have helped several clients calculate their moon sign who were not sure of their exact time of birth, but knew they were born within a two-hour window. So if this seems overwhelming, an astrologer can help determine your moon sign placement. Many people look at their official birth certificate, check their baby book, or ask their parents to find out an accurate birth time.

If you don't know your exact time of birth but know that the moon sign was moving into a new sign on the day and year you were born, you should read both moon sign chapters. See which moon sign traits resonate with you the most.

You can go online and calculate your birth chart on www.astro .com, or to just find out your moon sign, you can look it up on www.astrolibrary.org. You can also chart the cycles of the moon and learn more about it at www.mooncalendar.astro-seek.com.

DETERMINING YOUR MOON SIGN

When you calculate a birth chart, you will see a wheel divided into twelve sections. There will be colors, lines, and symbols within the wheel. To begin reading the birth chart, locate the numbers one through twelve on the wheel. These numbers signify the twelve sections, or houses, a birth chart is divided into.

First look for the number one, which will be on left-hand side of the chart. The first house is the beginning of the birth chart. Then look for the moon's crescent symbol. Once you've found it, look for the zodiac sign symbol that is placed on the rim of that house. For instance, in the sample birth chart, the moon is in the zodiac sign Aquarius. If you're having a hard time with this, many astrology websites have a section that clearly lists the signs and houses each planet is in.

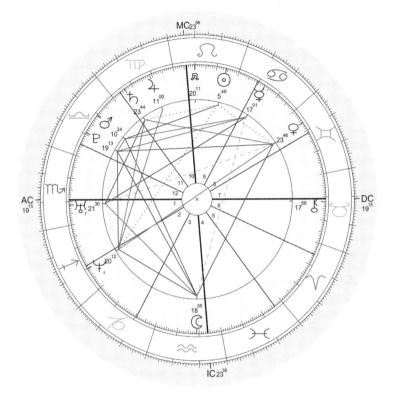

If your moon sign is on the cusp between two signs, you can read both chapters about those moon signs to see which fits you better. Emotionally, you might experience the energies of the sign the moon is moving into more prominently.

In the sample birth chart, the moon is in the third house. (We will be discussing house placements in chapter 13.) The moon might be on the cusp between two houses. In this book, if you have your moon sign on the cusp of two houses, you will want to read about both house interpretations.

THE MOTHER FIGURE

The moon represents the mother figure in astrology. The moon sign reveals the type of relationship you had with your mother figure and how you received nurturing. The astrological house the moon is placed in shows what types of experiences, lessons, and healing areas you have with your mother figure. It can show what challenges you experienced with her in the past and how you get along in the present. No one had a perfect childhood; astrologically, it's important to focus on the positive things your mother taught you about life, your emotions, and expressing yourself. Focus on her strengths and learn from her wisdom.

The moon placement often shows what psychic gifts and intuitive abilities are passed down from the mother or her side of the family. For example, my moon is in the eighth house. I benefited financially and emotionally from my maternal side of the family. My maternal grandmother was similar to me, although this was a secret for most of my life. We both shared an Aries moon, and we both dreamed of events before they happened. I discovered this about her when I was out of high school. My grandmother passed her gift of intuition on to me. Our maternal heritage and ancestry are associated with the moon sign, so you can learn a lot about your mother's family by understanding your moon sign.

Certain placements of the moon can reveal an absent or missing mother figure. The moon placed in the eighth house, for instance, can signify death of the mother at an early age. If this is the case, your motherly influence was often another female figure such as an aunt, grandmother, sister, or adoptive mother. If the moon is placed in the twelfth house, there is often an enmeshed relationship with the mother and a lack of boundaries. The relationship can be extremely close, but you might feel responsible for her well-being. It's common to feel like she is the child and you are the parent. Pay attention to the house the moon is in, because its placement shows how you nurture yourself and others.

THE MOON SIGN AND EMOTIONAL FULFILLMENT

Emotional fulfillment is a happy, contented feeling. It also represents a feeling of satisfaction for achieving what we desired. You might feel emotional fulfillment through work, achieving your dreams, having fun, saving money, traveling, or being a parent. The moon sign is a major piece of the astrological puzzle when it comes to emotional fulfillment.

Understanding your moon sign placement helps increase awareness about your inner needs. Each moon sign is unique and, in each chapter, you will be able to learn more about how you find emotional fulfillment. Looking at which house the moon is in helps you master activities that enhance emotional fulfillment in that area of life. Tips that will give you practical skills to implement will be shared in each chapter.

Everyone wants to be happy and feel loved. The key to finding happiness is to develop gratitude. Positive psychology teaches the more we focus on positive things in our lives, the less depressed we feel. Shifting our focus onto things we are thankful for helps us develop gratitude. Gratitude and happiness go hand in hand. To feel happy, you need to practice gratitude. Gratitude is the practice of focusing on the positive things we have in our lives. Appreciating the basic things in life such as food, water, shelter, family, security, good health, loyal friends, and adorable pets boosts positive feelings. Feeling happy, loved, and understood helps create a stable, rewarding, and comfortable life.

I remember learning a special technique when I took spiritual development classes. My instructor had us write down ten things we were thankful for. They could be material, emotional, or spiritual things. Some items on the list needed to be things we didn't have yet. The goal was to witness the power of positive thinking and the spiritual law of manifestation. After we wrote them down, we prioritized them from most important to least important to us. I found this encouraged me to have a more positive attitude. I also noticed it helped me feel better emotionally. Focusing on the little things in life that we often take for granted helps us realize how blessed we really are.

YOUR MOON SIGN SHOWS WHAT YOU VALUE

The moon sign represents what we value and the things that are most important to us. Each moon sign values certain things based on inner needs and desires. The moon sign provides the main compass that influences our ability to find comfort and stability. While studying psychology, one of the theories that resonated with me the most came from psychologist Dr. Abraham Maslow.

I have always felt that the astrological moon sign in our birth chart is similar to Maslow's Hierarchy of Needs theory. The moon sign is connected to our emotional needs; it represents what we need in life in order to feel safe and secure. Maslow believed people seek fulfillment through personal growth and change. He believed that some people seek specific needs based on their personality and inner desires. Self-actualized people are those who were fulfilled and doing all they were capable of while finding meaning in life. Every individual is special and unique and utilizes the needs pyramid in order to attain what they value.

Maslow's levels of needs are often shown as a pyramid. The most basic needs are located at the bottom and higher-level needs are located toward the top of the pyramid. I see a connection between Maslow's Hierarchy of Needs and astrology. After many years of counseling clients, I believe each moon sign utilizes a primary and secondary need in order to connect to and obtain emotional value. The moon sign and your unique values are tied together.

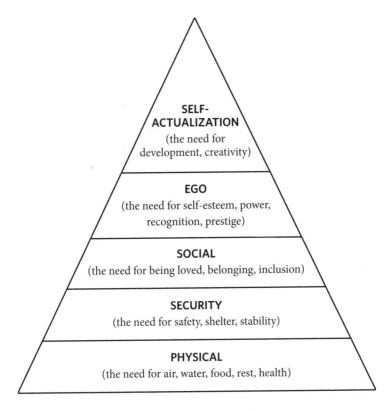

SELF-ACTUALIZATION
(the need for development, creativity)

EGO
(the need for self-esteem, power, recognition, prestige)

SOCIAL
(the need for being loved, belonging, inclusion)

SECURITY
(the need for safety, shelter, stability)

PHYSICAL
(the need for air, water, food, rest, health)

We all value physical and security needs, but some moon sign personalities focus strongly on those in order to function in the world. Some moon signs don't care as much about physical or security needs; they are focused on developing self-awareness, finding a spiritual path, giving up attachment to material possessions, or expressing creativity.

I believe astrological elements relate to these five levels of needs, primarily the element associated with an individual's moon sign. For instance, those with earth sign moons (Virgo, Capricorn, and Taurus) value physical and security needs because they require stability, security, and balanced practical matters in order to feel safe. Without these needs being met first, they struggle to maintain emotional balance. Air sign moons (Gemini, Libra, and Aquarius) tend to focus on social needs such as friendship, communication, and social inclusion. Fire sign moons (Aries, Leo, and Sagittarius) seek ego-based needs such as power, recognition, and success. From my research, I feel that water sign moons (Pisces, Cancer, and Scorpio) are more likely to pursue self-actualization needs and enjoy expressing creativity, spiritual development, taking care of others, and finding a higher purpose. In the coming chapters, I will discuss what each moon sign personality values most and will give examples of things that will help them achieve it.

MOON SIGN HEALING, TRANSFORMATION, AND RESILIENCY

The moon sign is connected to the heart. When we were children, we were more connected to our inner emotions and full of innocence, but life experiences and challenges can make us feel cut off from our heart centers and repress emotions. Developing a hard shell of protection is a way we protect ourselves from heartbreak, loss, judgment, and disappointment. It's your job to heal any issues that are negatively affecting your life. Doing so takes courage, strength, and resiliency.

In order for true healing to happen, you have to allow yourself to feel. To heal, you have to feel all your emotions. It takes courage to allow yourself to cry, feel unpleasant emotions, and process them. Everyone has wounds from childhood and adult life. We all experience difficult things. When we love someone, we believe they would never harm us, but the people we trust and love are often the very ones who hurt us the most.

Being bullied, lied to, or used by someone you cared about can leave emotional scars. Loss of a parent, friend, or loved one at a young age can reveal how fragile life is. These difficult life experiences can leave a lasting impact on your heart. A scar leaves a mark to help you remember. These memories make us stronger and more capable of developing greater resilience in the future. You can transform and adapt to similar situations in the future once you have the wisdom to overcome them.

To heal, you have to allow yourself to feel uncomfortable. Our moon sign dislikes feeling uncomfortable, but it's in those moments that we can heal the most. Talk to someone close to you, journal, or write out your feelings, and exercise in order to release pent-up emotions.

In this book you will learn how each moon sign heals, transforms, and finds greater resilience. Practical skills will be shared that can be used on your healing journey. Moon sign personality traits can be used to heal many areas of your life. Some moon signs struggle with healing the past and others heal more quickly. If you struggle expressing emotions, there are tips in this book that will help you learn how to become more comfortable. Expressing emotions and feelings is not a sign of weakness, but of strength. In this book, we will discuss each moon sign's greatest emotional challenges and information that can assist in healing any past traumas or unhealed areas of life.

FINDING YOUR PASSION

Our emotions are powerful forces that motivate us to fight, overcome life's challenges, and survive. Your emotional reactions, inclinations, tendencies, and urges come from your moon sign. The moon is associated with your unconscious and subconscious mind. It reveals what feelings lie dormant deep within your heart. Intense emotions are often hiding beneath the surface, wanting to come up. This is just like the moon: When you see the moon in the sky, it often hides behind the clouds. Then there are times you can see the moon shine through and show itself. The same is true for our emotional nature.

Passion is a strong emotion that we can have difficulty understanding. To be passionate means to have a zest for life or enthusiasm about something. Some people feel comfortable with their own feelings, while others avoid feeling anything at all. Your strong desires are linked to what you are passionate about. You may be passionate about achieving success, finding love, good health, or having children. In astrology, the moon sign represents your inner world.

Your moon sign gives strengths that are powerful enough to help you overcome any tragedy or loss. The moon sign is the primal part of our personality that takes over in a crisis. It's our fight-or-flight center that ignites the passion to move forward, and it gives us the ability to dig deep within ourselves, conquer obstacles, and embrace change.

HEALING EMOTIONAL WOUNDS

The moon sign and its house placement show where we feel most vulnerable. Unexpected change, loss, trauma, and crisis situations can leave a lasting impact on our inner life. Emotional trauma, pain, loss, grief, and emotional betrayal can be understood by looking closer at the traits of your moon sign. The house the moon is placed in will show an area of life where you suffered a wound. For instance, when the moon is in the eighth house, the individual often lost someone close to them. Eighth house moon people experience healing when they allow themselves to feel and process grief; letting go of the past helps them heal.

Every moon sign has strengths and weaknesses. We grow stronger when we allow ourselves to feel unpleasant emotions and face them head-on. Balancing our mind, body, and spirit helps us kick-start the healing process, and healing our emotional wounds helps us find greater happiness and emotional fulfillment.

Each moon sign experiences change and stress, so implementing self-care techniques will benefit you regardless of your moon sign. The goal of understanding basic moon sign traits is to help increase self-awareness. When you turn to the chapter on your moon sign, this book will shed light on your overall emotional nature, and I'll share tips that will help you connect with others. In the following chapters, I explain the basic personality traits of each moon sign. I also discuss each moon sign's challenging attributes, positive attributes, and how they express emotions.

These chapters are great tools for learning more about yourself and your loved ones. If you want to learn more about your family, friends, or coworkers, read their moon sign's chapter. In each chapter, I include moon sign affirmations, values, healing tips, and self-care ideas tailored to that specific moon sign. You can use these on your healing journey. In the final chapter, I will discuss how the moon placement in each astrological house impacts your life.

THE FULL MOON

Each month, the moon goes through a series of lunar phases. During a full moon, you will feel a multitude of emotions. Some moon signs will feel increased energy and motivation, while others may suffer from irritability, have difficulty sleeping, or become more emotional and depressed. When the moon is full, it has a strong influence on how we express pent-up emotions. Repressed feelings will come to the surface. Anything that is kept hidden is stirred up and brought out to be felt.

Each moon sign is affected differently by the full moon energy, and this has to do with the elements in your birth chart. For instance, the fire moon signs (Aries, Leo, and Sagittarius) will feel more energized, motivated to do things, and restless, whereas the water moon signs (Pisces, Cancer, and Scorpio) will feel a need to withdraw. In each chapter, I will discuss how the full moon influences each moon sign and share some tips on how they can work with full moon energy in positive ways.

MY OWN MOON HEALING JOURNEY

Now that we've covered the astrological basics, I want to explain why astrology and healing are connected. Astrology helped me heal and gave me tools to understand myself better. Having the moon in the eighth house in the sign Aries can be challenging. I feel things deeply and my emotional nature is intense. I was always sensitive, empathic, and compassionate but lacked the skills to protect myself. I had to learn to develop boundaries.

The eighth house placement of my moon brought many unexpected changes in my life. A friend of mine was accidentally killed when I was sixteen. This was my first experience with death. Emotionally, I was forever changed that day. I can remember every single moment from her funeral like it just happened yesterday. When I first started learning about astrology and my own birth chart, I felt comforted. When I first looked up "moon in the eighth house" and read the interpretation, it was then that my life experience was validated. The accuracy was uncanny.

As an Aries moon, I am naturally passionate and expressive about my feelings, and I had always excelled at sports and competition. Playing sports was a healthy outlet for my Aries energy. Playing basketball and group sports always helped me release pent-up emotions. But after gaining insight about my moon sign personality, I realized that I needed to learn patience. When I felt hurt or angry, I would repress it and hold everything inside. This created stress in my body, causing stomach issues, migraines, and overeating as a way to cope.

Writing and journaling have always helped me express my emotions and release them out of my body. Physical activity and movement help me release stress in healthy ways. Now, I try to incorporate walking and writing into my daily self-care plan. I make sure to calm down and take deep breaths before I share my feelings in order to avoid hurting anyone else. Healing takes time, so be patient. No one heals overnight—it is a lifelong journey.

Our moon sign helps us transform emotionally and become more resilient through experiencing adversity. I wanted to write this book to help readers understand their specific moon traits so they can use them to heal. While the sun sign is an important piece of our personality, I feel the moon sign has a greater influence on our ability to heal.

MOON IN ARIES

Nickname: Aries the Warrior

Symbol: The ram

Sun Sign Dates: March 21–April 19

Ruler: Mars

Rules: The first house; the head and face

Sign Type: Fire, cardinal

Polar Opposite Sign: Libra

Keyword: "I am"

Tips for Healing: Be patient, balance emotions, manage anger

Key Traits: Energetic, open to change, motivated, passionate, impulsive, impatient, domineering

Values: Independence, honesty, courage, physical activity, acting, achievement

Maslow's Hierarchy of Needs: Social and ego needs

Aries is ruled by the fire element. Full of passion and excitement, they see everything as an adventure. As a cardinal sign, they possess the strength of a leader. Aries moons are master negotiators. Courageous, confident, and brave, they believe they can achieve anything if they work hard enough. Overcoming challenges, fixing problems, and working in crisis situations are their fortes. Their instincts are strong, and they are often right, which is why they don't always listen to others—they trust their own emotions. They thrive emotionally when they experience stress, deadlines, danger, and conflict.

When the moon is placed in Aries, it creates a very powerful emotional nature. This moon sign is driven and expressive. Moon in Aries people express themselves in the moment and like action. They solve problems quickly; when they feel something, they don't like to wait around. Being patient is a challenge they need to overcome. They want instant gratification and tend to be impulsive.

Aries moon people make decisions based on pure emotion and gut instinct. Because of this, they can be emotionally headstrong, self-focused, and foolhardy. Sometimes they regret acting too fast. Aries moons should wait and allow their emotions to calm down before making important decisions. They would benefit from slowing down, thinking things through, and taking deep breaths before acting. Remaining calm can prevent unforeseen conflict.

Having a short temper and exploding in anger is common for Aries moon people. When Aries moons are upset, their voice raises; they communicate intensely and address anger in the moment. Then, once they've expressed their feelings, they quickly get over them and move forward. The problem is that others who felt the wrath of their emotional outburst are not able to forgive or forget as easily as they are. Aries moons move on quickly and emotionally push ahead to the next challenge, whereas other moon signs are still licking their wounds weeks after a run-in with an Aries moon.

Aries moon people instinctually offer quick, direct, honest, and straightforward communication in the moment. Thinking on their feet and making decisions based on how they feel comes naturally. This rashness can be a blessing and a curse, especially once they realize that others do not always appreciate directness. But if others try to slow them down, Aries moons can become irritated, frustrated, and rebellious.

I have my moon in Aries and realized the need to calm my emotions. If I am upset or frustrated, everyone can see it all over my face. Like many Aries moons, I dislike fakeness and superficiality. My facial expressions show my true feelings, especially when I am angry, hurt, or aggravated. Aries moons can't pretend they're happy with others when they aren't. If they are upset about something that happened, they want to communicate about it directly. Expressing emotions helps them release stress and negative feelings. This is why it is crucial for Aries moons to be able to vent with those closest to them, such as immediate family and friends.

Although Aries moons can appear self-absorbed at times, they truly care about other people. They are naturally gifted at motivating and inspiring others. Uplifting others and being seen as a supportive person makes them happy. And because they are emotional warriors who will fight for what they believe in, Aries moons stand up for the underdog. Protecting others and speaking for those without a voice comes naturally for them.

Having an Aries moon can be an amazing blessing that boosts confidence and belief in the power of love. Passion and relationships go hand in hand for this moon sign—without intense passion, Aries moons will wilt and become depressed. Sexual chemistry is crucial in their relationships. Aries moon people will cut ties and move on if they don't feel their intimacy needs are being met.

Aries moons need to feel wanted and enjoy being pursued by others. The thrill of the chase increases their energy levels. They are known as heartbreakers and lovers who like a challenge because once they get what they want, they grow bored and move on to the next obstacle. Learning to commit to others can be challenging, but it's an important lesson to learn. Aries moons need to be cautious who they develop relationships with, because unhealthy relationships can cause conflict and power struggles. Attraction to confident, charismatic, intense individuals is common.

Seeking adventure, conflict, and an adrenaline rush is common for an Aries moon. They want to feel alive. Warriors at heart, there is nothing an Aries moon will not fight for when they believe it's right. Taking up their sword and running into battle, always ready to defend gut instincts, is one of their greatest strengths. Aries moon people are the most courageous, brave, and energetic moon sign.

Aries moons need to trust their gut instincts and live life in the moment. Avoiding stagnation helps bolster emotional self-esteem. Romance, love, competition, and challenge help them thrive.

If an Aries moon had a mother figure present in their life, she might have had these traits, as the moon is the planet of the mother. Aries moon's mother figure was seen as independent, self-focused, and someone who had many hobbies. Strong, courageous, and driven, she was probably always on the go doing something. The mother figure might have been perceived as selfish. She had a strong, passionate nature and was brutally honest about what she felt. Aries moon people learn a lot from their mother about expressing anger and dealing with conflict. There might have been times when she was aggressive, either verbally or physically.

HOW THE FULL MOON AFFECTS ARIES MOON

Aries moons feel a buildup of stress and powerful emotions during a full moon. Heightened energy, feeling intensely motivated, and an ability to run on adrenaline to get things accomplished is common during this time. Emotions will be triggered easily, and Aries moon people can become short-tempered, irritated, and restless. The full moon awakens repressed feelings, and they come out fiercely. Aries moon people will benefit by watching the cycles of the moon so they are aware of how these powerful emotions impact them.

During a full moon, many Aries moons will experience unexpected conflict, arguments, car accidents, or disagreements. Medical emergencies such as accidentally cutting themselves with a knife, tripping, falling, and head injuries may occur more often during a full moon cycle. Lashing out at loved ones and arguments with spouses, children, and coworkers will be intensified. Aries moons should avoid conflict and unnecessary arguments by stepping back and taking a deep breath before acting. Learning self-control and patience will help them when experiencing emotional highs and lows.

FINDING PASSION

Aries moon is the most passionate of all moon signs; they are passionate about everything they do and are born with a natural ability to have fun.

Aries moon people are full of emotion, and finding their passion typically comes through relationships. Romance and being in love light their inner fire and bring excitement. They enjoy feeling new emotions.

Aries moon people need to feel appreciated and wanted. They enjoy being pursued by someone else from time to time. Feeling special is important, and having others shower them with attention helps ignite deep emotional needs. Chemistry in relationships inspires them and brings out their sensual nature.

Participating in hobbies they are passionate about helps bring greater happiness. For Aries moons, experiencing obstacles and achieving goals helps nurture an ability to connect with their passion. Seeking adventure and experiencing newness are all things that nourish their need for change.

FINDING EMOTIONAL FULFILLMENT

Aries moon people find emotional fulfillment through experiences that test them and make them feel alive. They like it when life is full of adventure, newness, and variety.

Aries moons require a lot of freedom and autonomy. As independent spirits, they need to feel free to make their own decisions. Emotional fulfillment comes from passionate relationships, but they need to keep a sense of self-reliance. Commitment can be challenging for Aries moons; they need to be allowed to explore. Physical affection is an important need for Aries moons, along with sexual intimacy. They feel emotionally fulfilled when they get to express their immense sexual energy with a partner who can keep up with their energy levels.

Being in charge, directing, and leading other people bring Aries moon happiness. Aries moon people desire recognition for the work they do; they need to be respected for their strong work ethic and amazing ability to get tasks done. Being appreciated motivates them to work harder. Full of boundless energy, Aries moon people can work and achieve things that most people only dream of. They're born with sheer determination to win, so being recognized for their great ideas and ability to lead others brings greater emotional fulfillment.

Showing anger and expressing powerful emotions helps them feel better; venting and releasing built-up tension brings a sense of peace. In return, Aries moon people like to be the one that other people turn to for advice and mentorship. Feeling needed is important, and there is nothing they won't do for someone whom they trust and respect.

Emotional fulfillment comes from experiencing affection, love, adventure, recognition, and success, and from working toward goals for the future. They have a gift for motivating others and are good at identifying what other people need.

ARIES MOON COMFORT

Aries moon people seek comfort by attaining their goals; having their needs met and being able to make their own decisions brings comfort.

While other moon signs crave stability, Aries moons need the opposite. Challenges and roadblocks inspire their lives and energize them. The more difficult something is for them to achieve, the harder they will work toward attaining it. If something is too easy, they won't be interested. Thrills, upheaval, and facing obstacles make them feel good. Stagnation and boredom create feelings of restlessness.

When life becomes status quo, being forced to follow strict routines and mundane predictability ignite an inner nervousness that hides beneath the surface. Having both change and comfort in their lives is critical for the overall well-being of Aries moons. They have a hard time sitting still and relaxing, but time for self-reflection and solitude can help them get in touch with their inner feelings. They have to make extra effort to take vacations and time off work, but releasing the need to always be moving around and doing something will benefit them.

ARIES MOON HAPPINESS

Aries moon people are happiest when they are reaching toward their goals. Being allowed freedom to be themselves and the ability to express thoughts, emotions, and gut instincts creates a sense of happiness. Feeling trapped or controlled by others creates frustration. They believe it's easier to do things on their own because it's faster, but shifting this belief helps them in the long run. Trusting others, making connections, and recognizing they do not always have to do things solo can create contentment.

Aries moons enjoy physical affection and being in love, and they're happiest when they are in intimate relationships. Having passionate desires met by expressing their sexuality makes them feel happy. Sexual compatibility in relationships and experiencing conflict in love motivate their powerful inner drives.

Playing sports and competing with others is fun and exciting. Being included as a key member of a team and leading others heightens Aries moon's self-esteem. Motivating other people helps them feel needed, especially because seeing other people grow and achieve their dreams makes them happy. Aries moons are enthusiastic and are happiest when they are helping others experience the excitement and spontaneity of life. Hearing positive words and encouragement makes them happy.

Making money, being successful, and achieving goals are linked to their overall happiness because Aries moons are competitive at heart. If they see something they want, they work hard to get it. Emotionally, they want to feel alive. They like to get stuff done quickly, and winning makes them happy. Aries moon people have an inner desire to be accomplishing things, and they prefer actions over words so they can see results.

ARIES MOON TRANSFORMATION

Aries moon people love change and excitement. Challenges and crises help them feel alive. The world is a place of adventure for them, where they can pursue and compete. They like to push themselves to the limit to see how much they can endure.

Aries moons transform when they accept that they don't need constant crisis and upheaval in life. It is second nature for Aries moon people to seek uncomfortable situations to feel inspired; stress encourages their inner drive to overcome anything in their way. The more challenging something is for Aries moons, the more they will push themselves to master it—they hate to lose and will do everything in their power to win any battle. Taking risks comes naturally, but learning patience before acting helps them grow stronger. Learning from past mistakes and realizing that impulsiveness can be destructive when it hurts others brings wisdom. By becoming more grounded and patient, they will realize they achieve much more in life.

Thriving during challenges and adapting to crises are gifts Aries moons possess, but they need to learn that depending on others is not a weakness, but a strength. Taking care of their own emotional needs is instinctive, but they need to be careful about being too absorbed by their own problems; transforming a "me-first" attitude helps improve many areas of their lives. Allowing those they care about to assist them and communicating openly creates vulnerability. Aries moons benefit from allowing family and friends to join them in life's adventures.

Passionate, with a drive to feel intense emotions, Aries moon people love romance. The feeling of being in love, the initial adrenaline rush and the feeling of being wanted by someone else, transforms their sensual nature. It forces them to focus on the needs of others and lessens self-centeredness. Affectionate souls who love attention, partnership helps them grow.

Aries moons are naturally born to transform every part of their inner life. Sheer determination and self-confidence make Aries moons capable of achieving anything they set their sights on. Transformation comes easily for Aries moons because their emotional energy is connected to the fire element.

ARIES MOON HEALING

Aries moon people heal by expressing their fierce emotions in healthy ways. Trying to control passionate feelings and being overly concerned about how others perceive them can get in the way of healing, whereas being assertive and speaking the truth helps encourage healing.

Aries moon people have emotional wounds that come from impatience. They tend to move on too quickly from uncomfortable feelings without processing them. Dropping people and moving on immediately from life situations doesn't give them time to process the impact, so unhealed trauma, regret, loss, and hurt feelings linger in relationships. They may find themselves repeating similar unhealthy relationship patterns or attracting the same types of incompatible people. Learning to balance their thoughts and feelings happens by remaining calm and taking deep breaths before speaking.

Others are caught off guard by the sheer amount of passion that Aries moon can express, but also by their selfishness. Selfishness is a way they focus within and protect themselves. Normally Aries moons are happy, easygoing, active, outgoing, and friendly. But the other side of the Aries moon personality is irritability, anger, frustration, depression, competitiveness, selfishness, and aggressiveness. Accepting these conflicting parts of their emotional nature helps them heal.

Healing comes when Aries moons can find healthy outlets to express their robust energy. Exercise is beneficial, and competitive sports or regular physical activity help them feel better mentally, physically, and emotionally. They would benefit from hobbies such as kickboxing, martial arts, basketball, or team sports. Exercising on machines or alone at a gym will be difficult for Aries moons because they like the social part of competing. Continuing to focus on their health, diet, and routine as they get older is important, as is balancing stress, because Aries moon people can burn out due to their high energy levels.

ARIES MOON RESILIENCY

Aries moon people are naturally resilient because they thrive on instability and chaos. I believe Aries moons are able to survive unforeseen crises better than other moon signs. Self-centered by nature, this personality trait is what helps them overcome obstacles such as loss and disappointment. Being a little bit selfish emotionally can bolster resiliency because they naturally focus within. They possess an inborn desire to survive, so they adapt to misfortune instinctively. Aries moons shift into survival mode and push forward. If they experience stress, an inner motivation pushes them forward, which enables them to overcome the darkest emotions. Aries moons' resiliency reminds me of Xena the warrior princess, grabbing a sword and rushing into battle screaming, yelling, and showing confidence.

Everything about Aries is fast: they feel quickly, act quickly, and charge forward quickly. This is one of their greatest emotional gifts. Brutally honest, direct, and self-assured, they always let others know how they feel. When they can embrace uncomfortable feelings like anger, rage, jealousy, and insecurity, it helps them attain greater self-awareness and improves relationships.

Aries moon people overcome adversity and obstacles easily because they know and understand the power of expressing things in the moment. They trust their instincts and inner voice more than other moon signs. Aries moon people never give up and enjoy proving others wrong. They like to win and possess the emotional courage to put everything they have into achieving their goals for the future.

Aries moon's ability to live in the present moment and be adaptable benefits them.

ARIES MOON VALUES

Aries moon people value independence and being able to make decisions on their own. Being able to act, feeling trusted, and not having to get other people's approval all increase personal satisfaction.

Aries moons are direct and straightforward, and they value honesty. They appreciate people who are trustworthy and speak the truth. When other people tell them how they feel, it means a lot to them because when Aries moons feel something strongly, they want to express it. They value good conversations and being able to discuss their feelings with trusted friends and loved ones.

Aries moons need movement and have a hard time sitting still. Boredom can lead to restlessness, and Aries moon people need excitement to feel alive. Aries moons have a willingness to take risks and step outside of their comfort zone. They are courageous, and when they believe in something, they are determined to achieve it. Aries moons value their own strength to overcome any obstacle.

Confident and self-assured, challenge inspires them. Being financially independent and having success is valuable to them. Working for themselves and owning their own business is their ultimate goal because they dislike taking orders from anyone. There is nothing more valuable to an Aries moon than being able to make choices based on their gut instinct and then act on impulse. They always have a feeling of urgency that affects their emotional nature.

Having to wait around, being restricted, or feeling stagnant causes stress and anxiety. Naturally quick at completing tasks, there are not many people who can keep up with their work ethic. The busier and more active they are, the better. They value making an impact and being recognized for the work they complete. Aries moon people value variety and being able to take on several projects at once.

Aries moons like to act and make decisions quickly. Thinking things through is not their style. They are known not to listen to others when they feel something strongly. But conflict, tension, competition, and change can motivate them to get in touch with their emotions. They trust their own emotions first and value self-reliance.

Aries moons are always aspiring to win. Hardworking, motivated, and energetic, they don't stop until they get what they want.

ARIES MOON SELF-CARE

Participating in physical activity, getting fresh air, and pursuing a favorite hobby are all things that benefit Aries moon people. Aries moons need affection and physical touch to feel happy; getting a massage of the head and face will help reduce muscle tension.

Spending time alone in the woods, surviving off the land, is a common self-care activity that many Aries moons enjoy. Survival is something they are good at, and proving to themselves that they can overcome all sorts of challenges motivates them to take better care of themselves. Doing things that give them an adrenaline rush—such as bungee jumping, mountain climbing, skiing, hunting, fishing, and sailing—are other self-care ideas.

ARIES MOON SELF-CARE PROMPTS

Aries moons can try to slow down, but most find it difficult to relax. Having trusted friends whom they can vent to does wonders for stress management because Aries moon people need to express their emotions. Journaling would help them express pent-up thoughts and feelings. Here are some journaling prompts for Aries moons:

1. Where do you find passion?

2. What makes you happy?

3. What moon sign traits make you resilient?

4. What helps you control your anger?

5. What makes you feel comfortable?

6. How do you handle emotional stress?

7. What is something positive you learned from your mother?

8. What self-care activities are you going to implement?

9. List three things that bring you emotional fulfillment.

10. List three things you are grateful for.

ARIES MOON AFFIRMATIONS

• "I face situations directly and take action."

• "I am self-reliant and strong."

• "I get things done."

• "I am patient and make good decisions."

• "I release feelings of stress in a healthy way."

MOON IN TAURUS

Nickname: Taurus the Stabilizer

Symbol: The bull

Sun Sign Dates: April 20–May 20

Ruler: Venus

Rules: The second house; the throat, neck, and shoulders

Sign Type: Earth, fixed

Polar Opposite Sign: Scorpio

Keyword: "I have"

Tips for Healing: Overcome stubbornness, embrace change, take action

Key Traits: Strong-willed, trustworthy, determined, affectionate, possessive, rigid

Values: Comfort, stability, commitment, peace and harmony, financial security

Maslow's Hierarchy of Needs: Physical and security needs

Taurus is ruled by the earth element. Taurus moons enjoy stability, sameness, and peaceful environments. As a fixed sign, they resist change. They are patient and like to plan their course of action.

Taurus moons have a very stable emotional nature. They express themselves slowly, deliberately, and patiently. When they feel something, they prefer to wait and think about what they should do next. Taurus moon people avoid chaos and conflict, preferring peace in all situations. Sometimes they stay stuck in the moment and refuse to act. Timid at times, they have to think about the consequences and make a plan before moving forward.

Because they are born with a natural calmness and grounded emotional nature, Taurus moons are able to be a great source of stability and support to other people. They give off a practical, down-to-earth vibe. Taurus moons are great listeners; they have a calming presence and an ability to ease people's anxiety. They are the most consistent people and are known to be reliable spouses, friends, and coworkers. Dependable and grounded, other people are attracted to their gentle, soothing, charming presence.

Taurus moons are artistic, comfort loving, security focused, faithful, and strong-willed. Taurus moon people like routine and avoid change. As one of the most sensual moon signs, they enjoy anything that brings peace, harmony, financial stability, and safety. Sensitive to sounds, smells, and textures, their senses are heightened. They love luxury and surrounding themselves with beautiful art, music, and aromas, but Taurus moons are learning to focus on things that are more meaningful than material possessions. They're also learning to value themselves. This is an important lesson Taurus moons have to learn.

Comfort and food go hand in hand for Taurus moons. They find pleasure through food, drink, and socializing with those closest to them. Emotional stress can lead to overeating and over-indulgence, which becomes an unhealthy coping mechanism. Using food to avoid unpleasant emotions stems from their need for comfort. When they feel sad, depressed, anxious, and uncertain, they bury these feelings; eating helps them numb their pain.

Change is difficult for Taurus moon people because it makes them feel off-balance. Taurus moons dislike being rushed or pushed to act too quickly. Taurus moons are creatures of habit that were born with a natural dislike for change. They dig their heels in and refuse to move. They hold on tightly to the past and stay where they are, often when it's unpleasant. Their anxiety about the future makes them rigid, obstinate, and sometimes difficult. Slow to make changes, they will not change for the better unless they embrace other people's advice. Single-minded, they often refuse to listen to those around them. It's important that Taurus moons learn to take other people's advice and open up their mind to other points of view.

Stubborn, strong-willed, and opinionated, they strongly believe in what they feel is right. No one can stop a Taurus moon once they've made up their mind. Their emotions guide their choices, and they will plant those hooves into the earth so nothing can knock them over. Like a bull in a china shop, sometimes they force their ideas and emotions on others to get them to conform. Focusing on being present in the moment helps Taurus moons grow, adapt, and prepare for change. Friends, family, and coworkers can become frustrated by their inability to listen and accept advice. Taurus moons often end up doing the exact thing that loved ones advised them *not* to do, but they won't admit they were wrong. It is difficult for them to apologize, and deep down, they like to feel in control. As an earth moon, planning and choosing their path makes them feel safe. They trust themselves first, and sometimes this prevents them from listening to others.

When worried, angry, or frustrated, Taurus moons need to talk to someone whom they can trust. Without this outlet, they repress their emotions. Because Taurus moon people avoid conflict and tend to repress their feelings, things can later erupt in a slow rage. Like a pot that is simmering for a long time, it eventually boils over. Taurus moons are slow to anger, but once they are aroused, everyone needs to be prepared. If a Taurus moon is upset, others will know it immediately because their face and neck will get red. They might raise their voice, which completely shocks others because it does not happen often; they normally dislike yelling and avoid loud noises. Taurus moons are known to sit and stew about things that upset them, but they avoid speaking up. Sometimes they get laryngitis or a sore throat due to withholding from vocalizing their feelings. Stress manifests in the throat, neck, and shoulders.

At heart, Taurus moons value peace and harmony. They feel nostalgic about the past, childhood friends, old lovers, and past memories. It's hard for them to release anything due to their emotional attachments, and living in the past can become part of their daily life. They repeat old patterns of behavior. Taurus moons are used to doing things their way, but sometimes this makes things more difficult for them. Releasing their need for order, structure, and stability can be scary, but they grow when they allow themselves to feel uncomfortable. Living in the past prevents them from moving forward. Hoarding behaviors are associated with unhealed emotional wounds. Many hoarders and individuals who have trouble getting rid of possessions have a

Taurus moon. If their material life is not organized and settled, they can't focus on what they need to accomplish.

The unexpected worries Taurus moons, and they don't like to feel unprepared. They are organized, rigid, and like to plan ahead. Financial success and having money in the bank for a rainy day help them feel in control. Taurus moons' physical needs are tied to their emotional needs; in order to find happiness, it's critical they balance both in their life.

My best friend is a Taurus moon, and she likes to plan everything and make to-do lists. She is the most patient person I know, and also the most long-suffering. Everything she values is connected to security for herself and her family. She likes to wait and think things through before making decisions. Avoiding the unexpected and feeling comfortable are more important to her than being forced to make decisions. She has a peaceful and calm nature that soothes others. Naturally affectionate, she likes to show her love by doing practical things for her friends and family.

If a Taurus moon had a mother figure present in their life, she might have had these traits, as the moon is the planet of the mother. Taurus moon's mother figure was a stable and calming presence in their lives. They perceived their mother as strong-willed, stubborn, and determined, but also as peaceful and calming. She may have struggled with letting go of the past and forgiving others; there was no way to change her mind once she made it up. The mother figure was seen as attractive, down-to-earth, quiet, and patient. Family, heritage, and structure were important to her, and the home was probably very cozy and comfortable.

HOW THE FULL MOON
AFFECTS TAURUS MOON

Taurus moons have a hard time repressing their emotions during a full moon. The calmness they typically feel can turn into restlessness. Taurus moon people hate feeling unsettled and uncomfortable.

During a full moon their patience is tested. Irritable feelings can bubble to the surface, and they are more likely to express them. Stubbornness can increase during this time, causing misunderstandings and disagreements with others. Their naturally strong-willed nature can intensify during this time, making it difficult to compromise.

They might try to hold on to old ways of expressing themselves, but heightened emotions need to be expressed. This might be the time each month that a Taurus moon allows themselves to cry. Allowing tears can be powerful in healing and releasing pent-up emotions.

Usually Taurus moons are slow to anger, but during a full moon this can change; during a full moon, their emotions are more powerful. Problems arise when their emotions start bubbling over and eventually erupt. Sometimes they feel an urge to verbally spar with loved ones. Their rage and intense emotions surprise those closest to them. Taurus moons might be more vocal about what is upsetting them, and those closest to them are not prepared to handle that. Typically conflict-avoidant, during the full moon they might seek to argue, bicker, and push people's buttons.

FINDING PASSION

Taurus moons need to experience physical and material comfort. Affectionate at heart, Taurus moons are sensitive to touch and need someone to cuddle with. They like to show people how they feel, so physical touch is important to them. In order to feel passion, Taurus moons must experience physical intimacy and fully trust the other person. Then, once their physical needs are met, they can let their hair down. Routine, structure, order, and sameness are things this moon sign needs in order to let go.

Taurus moons also find passion through hard work, planning, organizing, and being prepared for the future. Knowing what will happen and strategizing about plans helps them feel energized. Making money inspires them, and achieving practical goals makes them feel driven to do more. They are doers, but they prefer to go slowly, taking baby steps to avoid feeling rushed.

Crisis, instability, and change trigger stress and make them feel off-balance. Taurus moons need to learn to adapt to the unexpected. They need to trust themselves and others. They must release their need to always be right. Letting go of rigid thoughts and behaviors helps them connect with others in deeper ways. Relationships improve when Taurus moons truly listen to others. Learning to value others is just as important as valuing themselves. Other people's opinions matter, and Taurus moons need to remember that.

Taurus moons have two sides: one is practical, and the other is artistic. Expressing their creative side through singing, art, writing, and gardening inspires them. Once they trust in their artistic abilities that lie dormant, they become more passionate about expressing themselves in general. Taurus moons often set aside artistic talents due to feeling that these things are not valued by society. They feel artistic pursuits are not practical, which can cause them to neglect expressing their talents. Traditional at heart, it's hard for them to fully embrace skills that others might see as different. Making money from their creative endeavors can help heal these insecurities, but Taurus moons need to remember that money does not always bring happiness. They're happiest once they accept that they can be logical and imaginative at the same time.

FINDING EMOTIONAL FULFILLMENT

Taurus moons find emotional fulfillment when they can plan for the future. Making a schedule, mapping out career goals, planning for retirement, and having a set path brings them comfort. Taurus moon people struggle when their practical world is unsettled, unhealthy, or lacking a routine. Structure, relaxing surroundings, peace and quiet, and time to reflect can help restore calmness.

Taurus moons enjoy spending quality time with the people they love. It's important for them to share their success with their loved ones. In return, watching those they care about succeed—whether that is their spouse, children, or family members—fulfills them. They enjoy buying items for their children, pets, or partner. They also enjoy spending money on hobbies, the arts, eating out, and comfy clothes.

Success is extremely important to Taurus moons—it's part of what influences their self-esteem. Learning to love themselves even when they fail is a great lesson for them. They must remember that no one is perfect; you cannot always get what you want; and timing is everything. With time, they will slowly reach their goals through hard work and determination.

Ultimately, though, being prepared for the unexpected is critical for acquiring emotional fulfillment. Saving money and knowing they have a nest egg in the bank comforts them. Not having to worry about the future and having all their practical needs met is their goal. When things are going the way they planned, they feel peaceful and content.

Taurus moons like affection. Cuddling and holding hands helps them feel emotionally fulfilled. Expressing how they feel is easier through touch than through language. A pat on the back, grabbing your arm, and a warm hug are all ways Taurus moon people show they care. They expect the same level of physical expression from family, friends, and partners. The quickest way to relieve their stress, anxiety, and depression is to give them a big hug without them having to ask for it.

TAURUS MOON COMFORT

Taurus moon people feel comfort when they are able to relax, be lazy, eat good food, and cuddle with pets and loved ones. Surrounding themselves with people and things they love is important, and they adore not having anything to do except relax at home. Taking time off work is crucial for Taurus moon's well-being; experiencing career success and achieving financial goals they set for themselves helps them slow down and enjoy life more. They find comfort in saving money for a rainy day, but they should spend some of their money on a much-needed vacation.

Food is a major focus of Taurus moon's life. Not only does it provide sustenance, it soothes their soul. Many Taurus moons are foodies who love to try different restaurants and cuisines. Eating an amazing meal and having a glass of their favorite wine brings comfort.

Taurus moon's love language is physical touch. Without affection they feel unsettled and unloved. It is important that they pick a partner who can express affection through touch. Words are not as important to them because they feel that actions speak louder than words. If their partner doesn't share the same love language, it's important to find outlets for this need; cuddling with pets or friends who have similar values will bring comfort to Taurus moons.

Challenges can motivate Taurus moons to work harder, but they dislike disruptions that affect their routine. Stability, practicality, sameness, and being able to expect what will happen are key for overall comfort. Change creates stress, and crisis throws them off. They may not react in the moment, but they will need time to recover from the emotional shock of the unexpected. Doing outdoor activities also soothes them, especially gardening and putting their hands in the dirt. Some Taurus moons have a green thumb and surround themselves with plants and flowers.

TAURUS MOON HAPPINESS

When Taurus moon people are experiencing a balanced life, they are happiest.

Spending money on practical needs brings happiness, as does saving for the future. Taurus moons believe having what they need is more important than having what they want. Because they are hard workers, most Taurus moons will attain financial success. Their strong work ethic allows them to provide for their families. Surrounding themselves with beautiful artwork, musical instruments, and unique items makes them happy. Being ruled by the planet Venus gives them quite the eye for decoration. Some might be interested in interior design.

Having a trustworthy, stable, and supportive partner is crucial for their happiness. Taurus moon people need sensual touch such as hugs, kisses, and hand-holding, all of which make them happy. Physical touch is their primary love language and is very important in order for them to feel appreciated, loved, and happy. They are known to have a strong sex drive, and it is important to have a partner that can match their energy.

Taurus moons love eating, cooking, creating art, listening to or singing along with music, being in nature, gardening, and anything where they can be outdoors. Many of them like walking barefoot on the ground to feel the earth beneath their feet. They are grateful for the small, practical things in life. Happiness comes through feeling content, safe, and secure. When things are going well in their lives and their family members are happy, then Taurus moons feel their best.

Feeling forced to make decisions quickly and being caught off guard creates stress and disharmony. Having a plan and a step-by-step guide makes them happy. They are master planners, always thinking ten steps ahead of what needs to be done. Being able to choose when to act is key to their happiness. For Taurus moon people, maintaining stability and finding happiness are connected. Relaxing, planning ahead, thinking through problems, and helping those they care about are all things that make them happy. They are excellent listeners and enjoy providing a calm, safe space for loved ones to communicate with them.

TAURUS MOON TRANSFORMATION

Taurus moon people transform when they release the need to control every outcome. The future is often unstable, and life is full of change. Change is the most difficult thing for Taurus moons to accept because it makes them feel vulnerable, exposed, and unbalanced, but sometimes they need to have the rug pulled out from underneath them in order to grow. Some things can't be planned or controlled no matter how hard they try. Letting go is the answer. Taurus moons transform when they accept the fact that life is unsteady and that they need to live their life in the present moment, day by day. Releasing the past and forgiving others lightens their load.

Stagnation, stubbornness, and an inability to listen to other people's points of view need to be transformed. Taurus moons tend to repeat past mistakes by sticking to what they have always done, even when it is not the easiest way. Struggles come when they refuse to open their mind to other ways of accomplishing practical things. Instead of resisting other people's advice, they benefit from embracing a different point of view, even if it makes them feel uncomfortable. Relationships with others will improve when Taurus moon truly listens and takes other people's advice.

Taurus moons have to trust the Universe to provide. Thinking positively and avoiding dwelling on their fears will help them transform insecurities. Overcoming a thrifty, rigid approach to money will also help them grow. When they allow themselves to be giving and release their need for control, they thrive. Strengthening their faith in a higher power helps them let go of fear and uncertainty. Developing an optimistic attitude transforms many areas of their life.

TAURUS MOON HEALING

Taurus moons heal by expressing uncomfortable emotions in peaceful and loving ways. Quiet, calm, and observant, they dislike conflict. They don't always speak up when they want to or need to.

Learning to be more direct and sharing feelings with others—even if they are nervous—helps increase their confidence.

Food is used as a crutch to heal unpleasant emotions, and not addressing a problem can lead to overeating. Taurus moons tend to avoid taking care of their emotional needs; they neglect themselves and dislike reflection. But escaping from feelings only causes additional stress and potential health problems. Taurus moons need to release negative emotions in order to heal. Letting go and forgiving those who have hurt them is the quickest way to attain deep healing. Healing also comes from trusting others' opinions and advice. Taurus moon people need close friends and family to encourage them, even if they have a hard time allowing others to help them.

Taurus moons need more physical touch than any other moon sign. Hugs, kisses, and cuddles help them heal. They love being cozy! Taurus moon people often dislike hardcore exercise or physical activity; they prefer sitting on the couch, cuddling with their pet, and watching shows on Netflix. Being wrapped up in a soft, cozy blanket, snacking on their favorite food, and having alone time nourishes their soul.

Sometimes Taurus moon people get into a vicious cycle of weight loss and weight gain. Accepting and loving their bodies helps them heal. Their weight and self-esteem can fluctuate based on their mood. Some Taurus moons focus on a strict routine, while others use food to comfort themselves. The key is to find a healthy balance. Nurturing the mind and emotions is just as important as nurturing the physical body.

Finding time to relax is crucial for Taurus moon's well-being, but light exercise will benefit them as well. Being in nature is a healing activity for them. Healthy ways for Taurus moons to handle stress include walking outside, meditating, gardening, and writing. Laughing, letting go, and not taking themselves so seriously helps them heal as well.

Releasing material things and possessions that are not needed anymore helps expunge stagnant energy. Donating items such as unused clothes and shoes to thrift stores is something that benefits healing because it forces Taurus moons to release some of their attachments. Taurus moon people like to hold on to emotions, memories, and beliefs; this is a natural part of their personality, but they must realize when it's time to let go. Taurus moons must learn to forgive and release their attachments to the past. They will feel lighter and healthier by getting rid of things that are weighing them down—including their emotional wounds.

TAURUS MOON RESILIENCY

Taurus moon people resist feeling uncomfortable in any way. Being resilient requires overcoming unpleasant emotions and experiences. Trusting their ability to adapt to change will help them overcome life challenges. Expressing what they want and letting others depend on them is important.

Taurus moon people have a strong, earthy energy that helps soothe those who are suffering emotional crises. Because they are emotional stabilizers who help others feel calm, Taurus moons become more resilient by guiding others through challenging times. They are always seeking emotional comfort, and this trait helps them work hard to find a peaceful middle ground with difficult people. Acting as a peacemaker comes naturally to Taurus moons; they are masters of conflict resolution.

No matter what life experiences occurred in the past, Taurus moons are reborn when they allow themselves to feel. Forgiveness is key to their ability to become more resilient. They tend to hold on to the unpleasant memories of what others have done to them. Completely letting go of the past will morph them into the best version of themselves.

Overcoming adversity and unpleasant life experiences takes patience, and Taurus moons can easily overcome because of their persistence. Grounded, practical, and dependable, they don't give up easily. They have an innate gift of knowing what they need to do in order to plan for the future. Irritability, frustration, and negativity come out when they feel challenged and forced out of their comfort zone, but Taurus moon people become more resilient when they embrace the unknown.

TAURUS MOON VALUES

Taurus moon people value comfort and stability. Taurus moons' earthy nature needs a stable, peaceful environment in order to feel their best. Taurus moons value having their basic needs met. They seek out careers where they can make enough money to buy whatever they need. Money is power, and they realize having money helps them build secure foundations.

Taurus moons value financial security and material possessions. Having financial stability and enough money in the bank to provide for their family is top priority. Financial independence is invaluable because they dislike being in debt to creditors or owing anyone money. Ideally, they would have the freedom to enjoy the finer things without having to worry about losing their security. They like nice things but value thriftiness, because saving for the future makes them feel prepared.

Taurus moons also value socializing with loved ones. They need commitment in relationships. Having a dependable partner is important in order for them to feel emotionally safe. They find emotional stability by having a reliable partner, planning for the future, and practicing patience. They like things that are solid, lasting, and supportive. Taurus moons value commitment and are known to be fiercely loyal and devoted partners. They expect and need the same amount of loyalty in return. Many marry their high school sweetheart or someone they grew up with. Taurus moon people value their childhood memories, family history, and tradition; they are very nostalgic.

Chaos, conflict, and crisis make it difficult for Taurus moons to focus. They need peace and harmony in all areas of their life. They dislike change and like to have time to think things through before they act. Dysfunction, disorganization, and feeling rushed causes extreme stress—Taurus moon people value being able to do things at their own pace.

Taurus moon people need stability in every area of their lives and value it more than any other moon sign.

TAURUS MOON SELF-CARE

Taking time off work to relax is important for Taurus moons. Sometimes they neglect their own needs in order to achieve practical goals. Taurus moons should avoid overeating and try to limit alcohol consumption when stressed. Cuddling with their favorite pet, spending time with children, cooking an amazing dinner for their family, and listening to peaceful music are all activities that help them relax. To decrease the likelihood of being overwhelmed, Taurus moons would benefit from creating to-do lists. As they check off items, they feel relieved.

Spending time outdoors surrounded by nature helps ground their energy. Balancing body, mind, and spirit is important, but they might resist strenuous exercise or find it challenging. Yoga,

Tai Chi, relaxation exercises, stretching, or walking could be positive additions to their routine.

Spending time reading, journaling, and listening to music can be soothing. If they enjoy drawing, painting, or sculpting, they should make sure to carve out time for these creative hobbies. Expressing their creative side will recharge and reinvigorate them.

Taurus moons avoid unhealthy people, loud noises, and unpredictable situations. Peace, calm, and comfort are key ingredients in their self-care regimen.

TAURUS MOON SELF-CARE PROMPTS

Making time for self-reflection is beneficial. Taurus moon people need time to think before they act. Here are some journaling prompts for Taurus moons:

1. Where do you find passion?

2. What makes you happy?

3. What moon sign traits make you resilient?

4. What helps you embrace change?

5. What makes you feel comfortable?

6. How do you handle emotional stress?

7. What is something positive you learned from your mother?

8. What self-care activities are you going to implement?

9. List three things that bring you emotional fulfillment.

10. List three things you are grateful for.

TAURUS MOON AFFIRMATIONS

- "I am financially stable."

- "I am relaxed and in a peaceful environment."

- "Nature heals me."

- "I love my routine; it makes me feel secure."

- "I adapt to change and go with the flow."

CHAPTER

MOON IN GEMINI

Nickname: Gemini the Communicator

Symbol: The twins

Sun Sign Dates: May 21–June 21

Ruler: Mercury

Rules: The third house; the hands and lungs

Sign Type: Air, mutable

Polar Opposite Sign: Sagittarius

Keyword: "I think"

Tips for Healing: Rest, communicate feelings, find balance

Key Traits: Restless, intelligent, versatile, social, charming, friendly, witty, disorganized, unreliable

Values: Knowledge, change, fun, excitement, independence

Maslow's Hierarchy of Needs: Social and self-actualization needs

Gemini is ruled by the air element. Gemini moons are thinkers and communicators; talking and spreading knowledge comes easily for them. As a mutable sign, they embrace change and shift direction unexpectedly. Independent and social, they make friends easily because of their natural ability to connect to others.

Gemini moon people are emotionally adaptable, easygoing, and restless. Others perceive Gemini moons as unreliable and fickle. The truth is they get distracted easily and need constant movement. They move on quickly from projects, sometimes never finishing them. This happens when they are not challenged, emotionally invested, or engaged in the process. If they feel bored, it's hard to keep their interest. And when they do finish a project, it likely won't be done on time, due to their emotional and mental restlessness.

Gemini moons can be indecisive, and this is usually caused by overthinking. They don't like to choose one thing because they see the value in both. Geminis can find it difficult to quiet their active minds. Feeling anxious and unsettled is common. Many Gemini moon people struggle with nervousness and worry about future situations. Multitasking abilities help them focus.

Having mental stimulation is important for Gemini moons. They can juggle many things at once; they always have to be moving, thinking, exploring, or doing something with their hands. Born with high energy levels, they find it hard to sit down and relax. They change direction quickly and crave variety. There is an innocence, superficiality, and lighthearted nature that Gemini moons possess; they get excited about new projects, relationships, and hobbies.

Emotionally, Gemini moon people are juggling two distinct emotional natures: a sweet side and a disgruntled side—it's like having an angel on one shoulder and a devil on the other. They are always adjusting to their split emotional nature. Their mind and heart are connected, so their thoughts impact how they react. When they are not happy, they morph into a different person. They can be moody and struggle with irritability. Gemini moons catch people off guard with their sharp tongue. It's important for them to consider others' feelings before speaking. When upset, they lash out verbally for no reason; stress triggers this behavior as well. With that being said, Gemini moons usually snap out of bad moods faster than other moon signs.

Because Gemini moons go from one extreme to the other, they are often viewed as unreliable. Relationship partners might be hesitant to depend on them due to their changeable nature. But Gemini moons need relationships in order to feel happy. Talking about their problems with trusted friends and family helps them feel supported and emotionally satisfied. Being a part of groups brings emotional comfort because they dislike being alone. They are social butterflies, attracting many friends and acquaintances. People like them because of their sense of humor, openness, and ability to talk to anyone.

Born with the gift of eloquent speech, Gemini moon people have the ability to make others believe whatever they say. Communication brings emotional satisfaction because they crave intellectual stimulation. Telling stories, debating topics, and working through problems helps them express pent-up emotions. Witty and sarcastic, Gemini moons are known to have a wonderful sense of humor that helps them deal with unpleasant emotions and experiences. Other people appreciate Gemini moon's ability to make them laugh.

Gemini moons are naturally charming and sociable. Open and friendly, they are able to talk to anyone about any topic, and this stimulates their mind. There is an electricity pumping through their veins, always pushing them to seek knowledge and information. They are known to gossip and struggle keeping secrets. Impulsively spreading information makes it hard for them to hide their thoughts and feelings. And if asked what they think about something, Gemini moon people can talk for hours.

Chameleonlike, Gemini moons adapt to what others want them to be. They are good at pretending and mimicking other people's emotions. This may be because they feel cut off from their own emotions. Gemini moons might have difficulty talking about how they feel. At times, Gemini moons are unable to connect to their emotions, and this makes it impossible for them to verbalize how they are truly feeling. Emotional detachment is a common Gemini moon trait that leads to difficulties in intimate relationships.

Typically, Gemini moon's dual nature makes them attracted to two very different types of people, such as studious, intellectual types and strong-willed, emotional types. Juggling two lovers at once is common, as is loving two people at the same time. Settling down with one person scares them due to fears of losing their freedom. But they need to make sure friends and lovers are aware of the truth, especially when they are dating more than one person. If not, there can be tension and devastating toxic cycles. Commitment is Gemini moon's greatest lesson. Relationships can be destructive for them, so it is important for Gemini moon people to focus more on their heart center. With practice, they can learn to balance their mind and heart.

If a Gemini moon had a mother figure present in their life, she might have had these traits, as the moon is the planet of the mother. Gemini moon's mother figure was perceived as friendly, intelligent, and social. She was active, energetic, and always on the go. She had many friends, so entertaining in the home was probably a common occurrence. Education was important to her and reading was encouraged. She was an excellent communicator who loved to discuss everything going on in the world, and travel made her happy. She might have been more comfortable with words than with physical affection.

HOW THE FULL MOON AFFECTS GEMINI MOON

Right before the full moon, Gemini moons can experience difficulties falling asleep and staying asleep. During the full moon, they will feel more energized and unstable. Their mood can fluctuate unexpectedly and quickly.

Feeling connected to their inner feelings occurs during this time, although Gemini moons may feel uncomfortable with the increased intensity of their emotional reactions. They may regret expressing intense feelings but be unable to control their emotional outbursts. Gemini moons need to be cautious about what they say during this time—their words can cut others like a knife. Conversation will be riddled with miscommunication if they take out their frustrations on those closest to them. Relationship conflicts are more common during this time.

Anxiety and paranoid thoughts can plague them for a few days. They might feel on edge and easily agitated, making them appear more unstable and irritable. Rational thoughts can turn into obsession, making it hard to relax. They need to slow down and be careful about making rash decisions that could lead to injuries or accidents.

The full moon can have a positive influence by increasing Gemini moon's energy and motivation to get more projects finished. Their ability to multitask and complete unfinished projects increases during this time. They might feel more inspired.

FINDING PASSION

Gemini moons find their passion by learning as much as possible about other people. Interacting with people from different walks of life is exciting to them and prevents loneliness. Connecting with others on a mental level helps Gemini moons feel supported because, for them, passion is linked to the mind. As a result, connecting with people mentally will increase attraction and sexual chemistry. Friendship is a precursor to a physical relationship with someone. Often, friends become lovers because Gemini moons connect with people who intellectually inspire their mind.

Shared intellectual interests, a common educational background, and strong communication skills create bonds that bring out greater passion. Love is connected to verbal connection: if Gemini moons can't talk with someone easily, then there is no chance for romantic feelings. Talking is better than sex for a Gemini moon.

Gemini moons are seen as emotionally immature and unreliable in relationships. Casual dating suits them best, as they prefer to be free to roam and interact with people in the moment. If someone does happen to tie them down, it's because they connected with their mind, and that is something Gemini moons find hard to forget. Ultimately, they thrive in open relationships where they have the freedom to express their desires without fear of upsetting their partner or having to deal with feelings of jealousy or insecurity.

Socializing and entertaining connects Gemini moon people with a multitude of acquaintances and friends. The mental stimulation of a good conversation with an intelligent friend, sarcastic banter, and flirting all light a fire in Gemini moon's heart. With that being said, forced communication will send a Gemini moon running for the hills.

Gemini moons are drawn to things that are diverse and out of the norm. Meeting people who are smarter than them inspires them and challenges them in a way that they find exciting. Boredom and monotony are things that kill their passion. Traveling, visiting exotic locations, and trying new foods are ways to bring passion back into their lives.

FINDING EMOTIONAL FULFILLMENT

Gemini moon's emotional fulfillment is tied to their mental peace. If their thoughts are unstable, they will feel off-balance. Spending time alone helps them think through life issues. Reflecting encourages them to get in touch with what really matters. Taking time to slow down, turn inward, and relax does wonders to help them restore emotional balance.

Gemini moons have two distinct emotional natures that need to be balanced: restless and calm. Reading a good book, spending time at the library, and studying in their home office bring emotional fulfillment because they stimulate the mind. Playing games that allow Gemini moons to exercise their mental muscles, like chess and trivia, relaxes them. On the other hand, running around, darting from place to place, and staying busy also brings fulfillment. Gemini moon people feel like they should be doing something productive at all times. They push themselves physically, intellectually, and socially to stay active. Being in nature, hiking, canoeing, fishing, rock climbing, or any activity where they can get fresh air and use their hands brings emotional fulfillment. And they are a forever student, so taking classes in adulthood has positive effects.

Feeling free and having emotional independence is critical for Gemini moons to find fulfillment; possessiveness in relationships pushes them away. They need to be able to pursue what they want without worrying what other people will think. Gemini moon people feel emotionally fulfilled when their partner allows them to do things on their own. They enjoy flirting and meeting new people, and they appreciate partners who allow them to have friends of the opposite sex without feeling jealous or insecure.

GEMINI MOON COMFORT

Finding comfort can be difficult for Gemini moons. Comfort is not something they resonate with. Being too comfortable can feel confining and make them feel trapped. Superficial connections that are free from responsibility, heaviness, and commitment are more comfortable for them.

Gemini moons need constant change, new energy, and mental stimulation in order to relax. They do not know how to remain grounded; their mind is always churning, thinking about things to do, places to eat, or new hobbies to master. Learning and education probably bring the most comfort. Amassing their own library, listening to classical music, and finding new friends on social media can be comforting to Gemini moons. Being active helps them reduce stress and keeps them entertained. Sitting down and talking with those closest to them also brings satisfaction.

Gemini moon people struggle to understand the connection between their emotions and the physical world. Intellectual pursuits are more important to this moon sign than physical pursuits. Being seen as intelligent and having others appreciate their knowledge brings additional comfort.

GEMINI MOON HAPPINESS

Gemini moons find happiness in friendship and social connections. They feel happiest when others see them as funny, smart, charming, and interesting; they prioritize making people laugh and being liked. Deep down, they want people to like them.

Freedom, excitement, newness, and variety all make Gemini moon happy. Living in the moment and having the ability to jump in their car and go on a last-minute adventure without having to get permission from anyone brings happiness. Not having any commitments or responsibilities makes them feel light. Gemini moons are happiest when they are free to roam; they will never feel satisfied with stable routines and the status quo because they like to shake things up and experience change.

Gemini moons need to be able to change their mind frequently. When they work in a career field where they can research, uncover new information, and utilize their expansive mind, they will feel challenged mentally. Being able to learn new things, explore new hobbies, and test themselves creates a sense of growth. Avoiding boredom by doing two things at once makes Gemini moons happy.

GEMINI MOON TRANSFORMATION

Gemini moons transform when they learn to control the enormous amount of physical and mental energy they possess. Being present and in the moment helps them ground their energy. Slowing down, learning patience, and taking a deep breath before making important decisions helps them balance emotions.

Problems arise when Gemini moons have a full plate. If they can learn to focus energy on one or two projects at a time instead of juggling too many things, they will become more efficient. Sometimes they struggle to finish projects and leave several things half done; they move forward too quickly to the next exciting idea. Conserving their abundant restless energy and focusing it on what is important balances many areas of life and helps prevent burnout.

Emotionally, Gemini moons are like the Energizer Bunny, and they are capable of overcoming difficulties because they don't get too wrapped up in emotions. The only thing that gets in their way is overthinking. Learning to unwind, relax, and be less distracted helps them connect to their feelings. Gemini moons should practice meditation, focused mindfulness exercises, or breathing exercises to stabilize erratic thoughts and emotions. If they find it difficult to sit still, they can walk, hike, or spend time outdoors to connect within. When they control restless thoughts, they will be able to reduce stress levels and improve overall health.

Gemini moons transform when they become more reliable and follow through with promises they make to others. Proving that they can be trusted will help them transform relationships. Relationships also transform when Gemini moons avoid impulsive communication. They do not always have to be right—they can learn to allow others to be right once in a while. Giving others a chance to share their ideas first can help them become a better listener. Gemini moons don't have to be the smartest person in the room; they should allow others to get credit for their innovative ideas. They transform when they admit that other people sometimes know more than them.

GEMINI MOON HEALING

Gemini moons are prone to oversharing when they feel stressed or anxious, and they need to heal disruptive thoughts by getting to the root of the emotions causing them. Gemini moons should seek out a counselor or therapist who creates a safe environment so they are able to express themselves. Working with a trained professional to talk through the things that are bothering them allows them to vent in a healthy way. Learning to control their urge to blurt something out will help them avoid miscommunication and disagreements. Because they can be people pleasers and charm people with their words, Gemini moons must heal the pattern of telling others what they want to hear. Telling white lies in an effort to avoid conflict is something that needs to be healed. Communicating feelings directly and honestly takes practice, but Gemini moon people heal when they are able to openly discuss hurt feelings.

Gemini moons often feel lonely because most people are not on their intellectual level. It seems like they know everyone because they have many acquaintances, although, in reality, these relationships can feel superficial and lack depth. Long-lasting and true friendships are what they truly desire. Gemini moons heal when they form deeper relationships with others that aren't on the surface level. Finding one or two people that are just as smart as them and more practical will support their inner needs.

Healing relationship problems is important because Gemini moons often lack meaningful connections with other people. Boredom and restlessness lead to emotional difficulties, especially in intimate relationships. They need to heal traditional ideas about relationships that they believed they had to adhere to—finding their own path is key. Gemini moons resist commitment because they feel it leads to unhappiness. They move on too quickly from people, especially if they force them to commit. It takes a special person to catch a Gemini moon's attention and keep it. They are known to wander to greener pastures, but the grass is not always greener on the other side. Learning how to truly commit to another person in a romantic relationship creates greater healing.

It's crucial for Gemini moons to accept their inner need for freedom, independence, and excitement.

Sometimes people misjudge them based on their perceived erratic behavior. If Gemini moons learn how to ground themselves and take extra time to learn more about their feelings, they will heal. Developing greater self-awareness will help them learn to manage unstable emotions.

Reducing stress levels, practicing effective time management, and getting organized inspire healing. Practicing relaxation exercises can be helpful. Above all, Gemini moons need to embrace the mundane, practical parts of life.

GEMINI MOON RESILIENCY

Born with an extremely high emotional and mental stamina, Gemini moons continue to push forward after a crisis. Their adaptability helps them shift directions in order to survive. Typically, Gemini moons bounce back faster than other moon signs. This is probably because Gemini moons use logic to overcome sadness, and this trait can be useful in times of loss, grief, and upheaval. Thinking through challenges is Gemini moon's forte. They overcome unpleasant emotions by distancing themselves and keeping busy; being physically active and moving around helps distract their mind. But detaching from their emotions can backfire: if they distract themselves for too long and refuse to allow themselves to feel pain, sadness, anger, and disappointment, it eventually catches up with them.

Gemini moon people become more resilient when they learn to control their restless mind. When their thoughts are jumbled, pessimistic, and scattered, they can become irritable, depressed, and withdrawn. If Gemini moon people can become more aware of how their mind impacts their emotions, then they can put extra effort into facing problems head-on. Humor, laughter, and light-heartedness can help them overcome many trials. Wit and sarcasm can be a comfort during challenging times.

GEMINI MOON VALUES

Gemini moon people value intelligence and obtaining knowledge. They like to learn and study a variety of different topics. Taking classes and reading help them accumulate knowledge. They value being a subject matter expert in many different areas and pride themselves on knowing more about pop culture, art, and history than other people. When they do meet someone who knows more than them, they deeply admire that person.

Gemini moon people value having a variety of experiences. Having the independence and freedom to choose their own path nourishes their soul. They don't like being under another person's thumb—if they feel controlled, they will rebel. Acting on their desires is what Gemini moon people value most. Being forced to follow a rigid structure makes them feel claustrophobic, and they fight to break free. When Gemini moons get bored or disinterested, they might force change or shake up their lives purposely. They are drawn to a fast-paced environment because it makes them feel more alive.

Gemini moons are playful and like to have fun. They enjoy telling jokes, having witty comebacks, and making people laugh. They value a good conversation more than anything else. As such, they deeply appreciate strong and stable friends and partners who give them practical advice, especially because Gemini moons don't have the patience to be overly practical themselves. A person with a good sense of humor is valuable to them, and they feel comfortable around easygoing people. Flirtatious at heart, they tease people they care about—it's their way of connecting.

Gemini moons value communication and are inspired by good conversation. Debating and discussing topics with other people is where they shine. They can talk their way out of many problems and have a way of making it seem that their decisions are never wrong. If anyone questions them, they do not shy away from an argument or debate. Born with charm, they have a natural ability to convince others to believe what they say.

They make decisions based on their mood at any given moment. They are known for acting on a whim. Gemini moon people change direction at a moment's notice, which leaves everyone around them wondering what happened and scratching their heads. They like to be unpredictable and think on their feet.

GEMINI MOON SELF-CARE

Self-care for Gemini moons should involve some type of social activity, mental stimulation, and physical movement.

Gemini moons benefit from activities that help calm their active mind. Finding activities that slow their anxious thoughts helps them focus on what is important. Their restless energy makes it difficult to relax or meditate, though. Things like yoga and Tai Chi can balance their body, mind, and spirit. Spending time alone reading, writing, or playing games such as chess can be a way for them to unwind. Getting outdoors, enjoying the fresh air, and being near mountains, forests, or water reduce stress.

Exploring new cities, restaurants, concerts, and theatric performances with friends is stress-reducing for Gemini moons. Trying new things is fun for them.

GEMINI MOON SELF-CARE PROMPTS

Gemini moon people need a way to express their thoughts and emotions. Journaling and writing things out on a piece of paper can help reduce nervous energy.

1. Where do you find passion?

2. What makes you happy?

3. What moon sign traits make you resilient?

4. What helps you quiet your mind?

5. What makes you feel comfortable?

6. How do you handle emotional stress?

7. What is something positive you learned from your mother?

8. What self-care tips are you going to implement?

9. List three things that bring you emotional fulfillment.

10. List three things you are grateful for.

GEMINI MOON AFFIRMATIONS

• "I feel best when I share my feelings."

• "I know how to ground myself when I'm feeling restless."

• "I make time to pursue my hobbies and do things I love."

• "I accept that not everyone is on my intellectual level, and that is okay."

• "I focus on learning new things."

MOON IN CANCER

Nickname: Cancer the Mother

Symbol: The crab

Sun Sign Dates: June 22–July 22

Ruler: Moon

Rules: The fourth house; the breasts and stomach

Sign Type: Water, cardinal

Polar Opposite Sign: Capricorn

Keyword: "I feel"

Tips for Healing: Nurture others, prioritize family time, spend time at home

Key Traits: Protective, motherly, imaginative, sympathetic, moody, critical, possessive

Values: Family, comfort, creativity, trust, loyalty, helping others

Maslow's Hierarchy of Needs: Physical and security needs

Cancer moon is ruled by the water element. Emotional, sensitive, and imaginative, they feel things deeply. They are a cardinal sign, which means they like to start new projects, come up with creative ideas, and control the outcome of things.

Being ruled by the moon's energy impacts Cancer moon people greatly. Their emotional nature experiences extreme highs and lows. Feelings ebb and flow like the waves of the ocean. On one hand, they like to give love and affection to others. But they also have to feel appreciated, cherished, and protected.

Cancer moons are moody and more emotional than Cancer suns. They are born nurturers, but they sometimes block this caring part of themselves; if they have been hurt in the past, it can affect their ability to show love. Cancer moons can cut off energy to everyone and everything when they need to. They can be very giving or extremely cold, depending on their mood. They can be overly critical and controlling when they don't trust others; controlling behaviors can also pop up due to self-esteem issues. They can become clingy when they care about someone and are known to be possessive. Some Cancer moons have a reputation for taking things personally and being passive-aggressive, overly sensitive, and worried. Other people will instantly realize when they are upset because they can't hide it—when Cancer moons feel something strongly, their body language shows it. Many struggle with mood disorders, sadness, depression, and loneliness. When Cancer moons become moody, those closest to them need to be patient with them. Eventually, they will snap out of their irritable mood.

Cancer moons need time to process their thoughts and feelings. Writing, doing something creative, and expressing themselves are healthy and help balance out negative emotions. Doing something they enjoy, spending time with people who make them laugh, and surrounding themselves with positive people who are more adventurous than they are can lighten their mood.

Cancer moon people prefer to be around children and animals rather than adults. Children are innocent, genuine, and kind, which are all traits they resonate with. Cancer moons are born with a motherly instinct and often desire to have children of their own. If they decide not to have children of their own, they will find fulfillment working with children in some way. Caring for the sick or people who need help makes them feel useful.

Cancer moons are the best caretakers, confidants, and healers in the zodiac. They might be drawn to careers in the helping professions, such as nursing, social work, and childcare. Nurturing and taking care of others is a natural gift they possess, but they need to remember to make time to heal, recharge, and reinvigorate their own energy so they can continue to nurture the world.

Cancer moons can appear quiet, shy, and standoffish until they feel comfortable and trust others. Social situations can be difficult for them because they are introverts. They prefer small groups and spending time at home. Having time away from the outside world is where they find emotional stability: alone time and self-reflection help them balance their emotions. They value their privacy. They are easily overwhelmed by the energy around them, and cruelness, harshness, and unkindness can force them into their crablike shell. They feel intimidated by strong personalities and dominant people. Maintaining relationships and meeting social expectations can be draining for them, especially because Cancer moon people keep a lot of their feelings hidden due to fears of being hurt. They must learn how to take care of their own needs first. Turning down social invitations without feeling guilty helps them practice taking care of their own needs.

Cancer moons may withdraw and spend time alone for self-care, especially when their feelings are hurt, but they can become too isolated and push people away. Cancer moon people prefer one or two close friends and avoid large groups. They are extremely protective of friends and family. Sometimes they might only have one close friend and put a lot of pressure on that person to spend time with them. Cancer moons need to accept that family and friends have other responsibilities and other relationships in their lives. Releasing their grip on other people and allowing others to have freedom without feeling abandoned is a learning lesson.

Family and loyalty mean everything to Cancer moons, and they will sacrifice comfort to provide for loved ones. Cancer moons speak up for others and defend people they care about but have a hard time speaking up for themselves. They enjoy helping friends, taking care of people, and lessening the emotional pain of those around them if they can. But Cancer moon people have to feel comfortable in order to show emotions in return. Relationships are very important to them, but they are particular about who they trust. If they don't feel safe, they can shut off their emotions, retreat, and withhold love from others. Accused of being cold at times, they can withdraw affection easily when they feel hurt or disappointed.

If Cancer moons have a choice between staying home or going out, they will choose staying home every time. But getting out of the house sometimes is good for their emotional balance! The home is Cancer moon's castle, and they ensure their home is a peaceful, beautiful, comfortable, and safe place. They need to withdraw into their home just like crabs withdraw into their hard shell. It takes them a long time to trust others or invite people into their inner sanctuary—if they invite you into their home, it means you are accepted into their inner circle. Feeling safe and secure in the comfort of their own home and far away from other people is how they cope with stress. Those closest to Cancer moons need to accept that the home is where they feel most comfortable and where they can be themselves. Cooking dinner in the kitchen, socializing in the living room, and cuddling with a pet while watching a good movie is the perfect date night for a Cancer moon.

My husband is a Cancer moon, and after twenty-three years of marriage, he is someone who likes to be home. He prefers spending time at home with me and our daughter or by himself in our basement. He cares about people, but having to put effort into relationships is emotionally draining for him. There are times when he struggles to express how he is feeling; Cancer moon people have deep feelings but struggle to find the right words. Naturally shy, they tend to observe situations before they speak, and they need to feel comfortable in order to express vulnerability.

Cancer moons remember everything and have excellent memories. Because they are inherently connected to the past, memories of their parents, childhood experiences, neighbors, and friends are important to them. They spend a lot of time reminiscing about past hobbies, achievements, and people they loved. They collect things and have a hard time releasing memories, which is similar to how Taurus moons feel. They like to hold on to things because their memories become a part of their soul, connecting them to loved ones.

Because they absorb other people's emotions, Cancer moons have increased feelings of depression, sadness, and irritability. It is important for them to utilize their shell of protection when they need it. Developing boundaries will help them balance their emotional reactions.

Cancer moons and Virgo moons are the two worriers of the zodiac: Virgo moon's worry is intellectual and Cancer moon's worry is emotional. They worry about their health and their loved one's safety. Known to be hypochondriacs, they want to know what is happening and make sure everyone is eating a balanced meal, has clean clothes to wear, and is practicing a healthy routine. Negative emotions can affect their health and cause stomach problems.

Cancer moon people rely on their feelings and make decisions based on an inner knowing. The moon rules over the sign Cancer, and therefore the moon's energy is comfortable expressing itself here. As a result, Cancer moons are blessed with intuitive abilities. They are born with heightened sensitivity to the environment, so Cancer moon's gut instincts are always spot on. Cancer moons should always trust their intuition because it protects them from dangerous situations.

If a Cancer moon had a mother figure present in their life, she might have had these traits, as the moon is the planet of the mother. Cancer moons are very connected to their mother and female figures. Their childhood experiences impacted and molded their personality. Cancer moons experienced their mother as nurturing, protective, possessive, controlling, depressed, and sometimes cold. At an early age, being taught how to show love was an important lesson; the mother figure bond needs to be positive in order for Cancer moons to experience intimacy later in life. Cancer moon people learn a lot from their mother, and if this relationship is healthy, it can last well into old age. If the mother figure was absent or not supportive, it can negatively affect Cancer moon's ability to open up. Some Cancer moons find themselves feeling responsible for their mother's emotional and financial stability. They often step in to care for her when she grows older.

HOW THE FULL MOON
AFFECTS CANCER MOON

Cancer moons might feel more energized, comfortable, and grounded when the moon is full. Typically, they experience positive energy and happier emotions. An increased desire to nurture and take care of others is common during this time.

On the other hand, Cancer moons may experience emotional disruptions or unstable feelings during the full moon. Emotions are deep during this time, and it can be difficult to know how to express them. They might feel more moody, sad, or cry more easily. There can be an increased desire to withdraw from everything and stay home even more than usual. Insomnia can be common during this time, as can oversleeping.

This is a good time to reflect on things from the past. Forgiving others and letting go of old hurt will help Cancer moons move forward.

FINDING PASSION

Cancer moons are worriers. Worries revolve around security concerns such as potential financial problems, losing their job, their family's well-being, and health problems. This trait prevents them from pursuing their dreams or taking risks. Letting go of fears of failure, disappointment, and shyness will help them find their passion.

Passion is associated with feeling safe, comfortable, and needed. Helping others in some way and nurturing those who need love bring Cancer moons joy. Passionate about standing up for people who can't speak up for themselves, they are drawn to social work and counseling fields where they can support others in need. Being of service ignites an inner passion because they want to make a difference in the world. When they feel appreciated for their natural caretaking abilities, there is nothing they wouldn't do for someone. Feeling needed by others inspires them to work harder and energizes them.

When Cancer moons feel in control of their lives, they can build a comfortable home base. Having stability in the home is connected to their energy level and ability to enjoy life. Spending time cleaning, cooking, straightening the house, or planning family activities is what Cancer moons do best. Spending time with a handful of trusted friends in a calm, peaceful, and supportive home environment motivates their creative passion.

Expressing their creativity in various ways is important. Many Cancer moons enjoy writing, art, music, and theater. Talented, imaginative, and caring, they are able to express feelings through creative pursuits. Getting in touch with their deeper emotions helps them find their inner passion.

FINDING EMOTIONAL FULFILLMENT

Cancer moon's emotional fulfillment is connected to their family. Supporting their spouse, children, siblings, and parents is fulfilling. Family comes first for Cancer moons. Genealogy interests them because they enjoy finding out more about their ancestors and heritage. Because they are nostalgic at heart, family traditions bring emotional fulfillment and are a way for Cancer moons to carry on important family rituals.

It's important for Cancer moon people to find ways to balance their insecurities, overcome jealousy, and eliminate controlling behaviors. Intimate relationships and love can bring emotional fulfilment, but trust is key.

Alone time, solitude, and peaceful surroundings enhance fulfillment. Privacy, seclusion, and quality time to withdraw soothe their soul.

Worry can make it hard for Cancer moons to feel emotionally fulfilled and grounded. Trusting the Universe helps them let go of insecurities, fears, and pessimistic thinking. Unstable emotions affect their mind, so it's important to keep a positive outlook.

CANCER MOON COMFORT

Cancer moon people are known to experience emotional extremes due to being a water sign. Just like the tides of the ocean, their mood fluctuates. Balancing pessimistic tendencies and managing stress helps them find contentment and inner satisfaction. Seeking comfort is a way to focus on stabilizing their powerful feelings. When the tides are calm within, then Cancer moons can feel comfort outside themselves in the real world.

Cancer moons need time to rest, relax, and surrender. They try to maintain comfort by escaping and withdrawing from the world. Being able to stay home, doing whatever they want, brings inner peace. They also find comfort in knowing their family is safe and supported.

Cancer moons are the epitome of comfort and always strive to feel safe, secure, calm, and peaceful. Emotional comfort is connected to practical security; Cancer moons need both these areas to be balanced in order to feel comfortable.

CANCER MOON HAPPINESS

Cancer moons are happiest when they receive affection and support from others. Trusting others with their heart is an important lesson for Cancer moons because their happiness is tied to allowing others into their inner world, which means they have to overcome fears of being vulnerable. It can feel burdensome to always distrust or doubt others' intentions; coming out of their outer shell of protection is something that ultimately brings greater happiness.

Taking care of family, children, and animals makes Cancer moon people happy, but learning to take care of their own needs is an important lesson to learn. They also feel happy when others take care of them without them having to ask.

Stress influences their emotional nature more than it affects other moon signs. Cancer moon's dream situation in life is one where they do not have to struggle with security. Having financial security helps them feel safe and supported.

CANCER MOON TRANSFORMATION

Cancer moons transform when they stop worrying about everything that can go wrong. Having greater faith in people helps them grow. Putting their faith in a higher power and developing a spiritual path helps them embrace change.

Cancer moons tend to obsess and fret over everything that can go wrong; controlling things helps them feel prepared for situations that might personally impact their lives. But the Universe supports Cancer moons when they go with the flow and allow themselves to look forward to the future. Self-fulfilling prophecies are real and can impact daily life. Cancer moon's thoughts and emotions are connected. If they can shift their feelings and thoughts in a positive way, it helps decrease fears of the unknown. They will manifest things they want and avoid things they are afraid of.

Living in the past keeps them stuck, so Cancer moon people transform when they move forward with greater hope. Letting go of unpleasant memories will help them transform many areas of their lives. Forgiving parents, siblings, and friends for any mistreatment that occurred in childhood helps them change negative patterns. Healing familial karma will help them grow and flourish as an independent person.

Protecting themselves comes naturally and is a defense mechanism used to overcome challenges. But hiding in their home and refusing to spend time in social situations can make them feel more despondent and isolated. Isolation can increase feelings of depression, sadness, and worry. Naturally shy, trusting others with their feelings is difficult. Allowing caring people into their life helps them transform into a more trusting, compassionate, caring, and understanding person.

Cancer moons can push others away if they smother them too much. Acknowledging the fact that they don't always have to mother everyone or take care of others' needs first helps Cancer moon people find strength.

CANCER MOON HEALING

Cancer moons heal by spending time alone in solitude. Taking time to reflect on their emotions helps them move forward from loss, grief, tragedy, and change. Writing and journaling can help them expunge traumatic emotions from their body. Family karma and past-life cycles related to nurturing and mothering impact Cancer moon's healing. Releasing old wounds and disappointments caused by people they cared about is important in order for Cancer moons to truly heal. Adjusting current emotional expectations for their family spurs healing and growth.

Letting down the hard shell that protects their soft interior can encourage Cancer moon people to step out of their comfort zone, which ignites greater healing. Pushing themselves to take risks and be vulnerable increases their ability to trust others. Sharing deep feelings with someone they care about leads to greater intimacy and fulfillment. Allowing people to help them can be extremely healing for Cancer moons. Taking care of everyone else is second nature, but they heal when they learn to make themselves a priority.

Spending time near any type of water is healing. Soaking in a hot tub, bathing in a bubble bath, swimming, and allowing water to cleanse them helps them feel better.

CANCER MOON RESILIENCY

Cancer moon's crablike shell is one of the things that makes them resilient; it enables them to keep out negative people and protect their inner sanctuary, which is their heart. But being comfortable at all costs can block growth—Cancer moons need to embrace the unknown. Trusting their own inner voice helps them overcome many obstacles. Cancer moons are known to have amazing intuition and can use their spiritual gifts to find answers. Their gut instincts are rarely wrong; they are one of the most intuitive moon signs. They need to acknowledge and embrace their psychic abilities and creative gifts.

Trusting the process of life and other people inspires greater resiliency. Cancer moons grow stronger when they release the vise grip they have on others. They will have an "aha" moment when they recognize people must *choose* to be in their lives; trying to control other people only pushes them further away. They become more resilient when they release their attachment to people and material things.

CANCER MOON VALUES

Cancer moon people value family, heritage, and tradition. They enjoy doing things for their loved ones, such as cooking, cleaning, and taking care of family members; kindness, sensitivity, and loyalty are important to them. Cancer moons feel a sense of responsibility for their mother, and they value that relationship. Spending quality time with family in the comfort of their own home is a priority. Some Cancer moons even invite their parents to move in so they can take care of them. Caretakers at heart, helping those in need comes naturally.

Cancer moon people are empathic and can put themselves in others' shoes. When loved ones are struggling with stress, insecurities, and anxiety about the unknown, Cancer moons like to provide a calming influence. They enjoy providing a listening ear, and they can offer practical advice and solutions to others' problems.

Naturally cautious and protective, they get attached once someone touches their heart. But being able to trust someone is a huge step for Cancer moons. It takes them a long time to believe others are worthy of their friendship. Cancer moons are protective of and faithful to those they love. They value quality over quantity in relationships.

CANCER MOON SELF-CARE

Spending time alone in the comfort of their own home is how Cancer moons nurture themselves. Moments of solitude, feeling cozy, and having a good work-life balance are all critical components of Cancer moon's self-care regime. They value peace, comfort, and harmony in all areas of their life. Putting on their pajamas, cuddling with their favorite pet, reading a good novel, and sipping tea is more important to them than going out. Solitude allows Cancer moons to process their emotions; tapping into deep feelings and expressing them alleviates stress. Taking time away from social pressures and commitments enables them to think clearly.

As the most emotional moon sign, Cancer moons struggle with compassion fatigue. Learning when to say no and taking breaks helps Cancer moons learn their own limits. They can't adequately take care of others if they neglect their own needs! Developing strong boundaries is important for their overall mental health.

Making time for creativity is beneficial and rewarding, and it is a way for Cancer moon people to express their innermost feelings. They can connect with their emotions through writing, making art, or listening to music. Many Cancer moons have artistic talents and can make a living doing something creative. If they have trouble tapping into their artistic side, walking, playing with children, and meditating are good hobbies to pursue.

Spending time near water is also healing for Cancer moons. Water cleanses negative energy and replenishes the body. Cancer moon people should take bubble baths, soak their feet in the ocean, and make sure they drink enough water. Swimming, water aerobics, and riding in a boat are other beneficial activities.

CANCER MOON SELF-CARE PROMPTS

Journaling and expressing their feelings in writing can relieve anxiety and be beneficial for Cancer moons.

1. Where do you find passion?

2. What makes you happy?

3. What moon sign traits make you resilient?

4. What helps you trust your intuition?

5. What makes you feel comfortable?

6. How do you handle emotional stress?

7. What is something positive you learned from your mother?

8. What self-care tips are you going to implement?

9. List three things that bring you emotional fulfillment.

10. List three things you are grateful for.

CANCER MOON AFFIRMATIONS

- "I recharge when I spend time at home."

- "Solitude helps me feel grounded."

- "I utilize my imagination and creative gifts."

- "Water heals me."

- "I listen to my intuition and trust my inner voice."

Moon in Leo

Nickname: Leo the Performer

Symbol: The lion

Sun Sign Dates: July 23–August 22

Ruler: Sun

Rules: The fifth house; the heart and spine

Sign Type: Fire, fixed

Polar Opposite Sign: Aquarius

Keyword: "I will"

Tips for Healing: Seek pleasure, be affectionate, express yourself, prioritize social connections

Key Traits: Proud, artistic, dramatic, dominant, self-centered, charming

Values: Independence, recognition, status, passion, playfulness, social connections

Maslow's Hierarchy of Needs: Social and ego needs

Leo is ruled by the fire element. Leo moon people are social, energetic, and charming. As a fixed sign, they want things done a certain way; when they believe they are right, no one can change their mind. Strong-willed and stubborn, they resist change unless they choose to do something themselves. As natural leaders, they like to take charge and want others to follow.

Leo moons are expressive and creative. Blessed with artistic, athletic, and musical abilities, they are very talented. They excel at anything they put their whole heart into. Leo moons do not always realize they have artistic talents. Their innate gifts are there, but sometimes it takes other people to pull them out.

Leo moons enjoy being in the limelight. They have larger-than-life personalities and attract many friends. They are brave, courageous, and affectionate, and they know how to have a good time. Being the center of attention comes naturally because there is a confidence that surrounds Leo moons; they are boisterous, loud, social, and entertaining, yet they make others feel at ease with their generous nature. It doesn't take much for them to begin entertaining large groups of people. People are attracted to their warm and bright energy.

Free-spirited, independent, happy, joyful, and confident, Leo moons make good friends. Spending time socializing, telling jokes, eating, drinking, and having fun helps them relax and overcome stress. Sure, their superficial charm enables them to connect with everyone easily, but lasting, true friendships are special to them because it is difficult to find people they can confide in. When someone touches their heart, a Leo moon will do anything for them. Even though they appear strong, they have a sentimental side. Those closest to Leo moons feel their warmth, especially because they have a huge heart. Giving their energy and time to those they care about comes naturally. Leo moon people are generous and enjoy giving people they love gifts. They're also very protective, and their friends become like family to them. Loyalty is important in order for them to connect to others in a deep way.

Because they are passionate, confident, and sophisticated, Leo moon people attract romance. They're flirtatious and enjoy love affairs. Finding a partner who is just as strong as them is helpful; they won't be attracted to someone who appears weak. They are attracted to people like them: confident, intelligent, and creative. Partnering with more organized and detail-oriented people would be beneficial. Leo moons also appreciate lovers who can help them relax and enjoy life.

Leo moons are extremely dedicated to people they care about. They are sometimes self-absorbed and focused only on what they think, want, and need. With that being said, they want to feel free to roam and have independence. They don't like feeling trapped or stifled. Having the power to make their own decisions in life is crucial. If they can find a partner who doesn't restrict their freedoms in a relationship, they will be more likely to commit. Excitement, fun, and adventure keep them interested in relationships. Once a Leo moon loves someone, it will be difficult for them to hide it. Leo moon people are very expressive with their feelings. They find it easy to let others know how they're feeling about them and are loving partners. They can get a bad reputation for not being monogamous. They love attractive people and are flirtatious. Making commitments in relationships can be challenging for them.

Leo moons are children at heart and enjoy being parents. Leo moons make nurturing, caring, and supportive parents. They believe their children are special and that other children are not as talented as their own. Leo moons are attentive to their children's needs. But giving their children everything they want can lead to parenting difficulties—they have to learn boundaries and enforce rules. They sacrifice for their children and like to advocate for the rights of all children. If they don't have children of their own, they will enjoy working with children, being an aunt or uncle, or volunteering to help children in need. Some Leo moons are drawn to teaching. Their students love them, and this attention soothes their soul.

I have several Leo moons in my life. They have a quiet confidence that shines through and a great sense of humor. Strong and kind at the same time, they are happy and high-energy people. One friend of mine who has a Leo moon told me that his mother was the most important person in his life. A college friend of mine with a Leo moon was always seeking supervisory positions where she could have authority to make decisions. She enjoyed supervising people and being a leader. Challenge, conflict, and change in the work environment were exciting for her. Strong-willed, she did not want to be told what to do. She needed to be in a management position where she had oversight over other people. Giving orders was easier for her than following others.

Being in a position of power makes Leo moons feel emotionally content. They make natural leaders because they understand what people want and have the ability to socialize with people from all walks of life. Leo moons are good at leading others toward shared goals. They naturally see the bigger picture and believe anything is possible. They recognize power in others and know how to get close to important people. Leo moons use their social connections to influence their career.

Leo moon people want to feel needed and appreciated. They like being seen as strong, confident, and authoritative. And they expect a certain level of special treatment—after all, they *are* associated with royalty. Being respected and valued for their opinion is important to Leo moons. They only want to associate with people who understand them and treat them with respect. Many excel quickly and move up the ladder in their early years. Driven to succeed, they charm others and utilize social connections to get what they want.

Performing on a stage in front of an audience makes them feel special. Typically, Leo moon people enjoy acting, entertaining, and activities that help with self-expression. It's important for Leo moons to express themselves, though it can be done in subtle ways. Leo moons who are more introverted might find it difficult to express themselves in front of a large crowd and prefer to write, play an instrument, or create art in the privacy of their own home.

If a Leo moon had a mother figure present in their life, she might have had these traits, as the moon is the planet of the mother. Leo moons may have perceived their mother figure as domineering, artistic, successful, confident, and focused on herself. Their mother might have been in the public eye or worked in a career such as acting, performing arts, or politics. Leo moons often cherish their mother and believe she is special. From an early age, the mother figure was someone they looked up to. As Leo moons grew older, they began to seek out relationships with individuals who reminded them of their mother. Leo moons put their mother on a pedestal and see her as important. No one is as beautiful, loving, or revered as their own mother. They learned a lot about expressing themselves and showing affection from their mother, so if the mother figure was self-focused or neglectful, Leo moons can struggle with self-esteem issues and a lack of confidence.

HOW THE FULL MOON
AFFECTS LEO MOON

Leo moons feel more emotional, restless, and unsettled during a full moon. Experiencing a lack of energy and not feeling as social as usual is common for Leo moons. They are more sensitive during this time and may take things personally. Overreacting can cause conflict. Leo moon's ego can get hurt much easier during a full moon. They might seek more attention from family and friends during this time. If they feel lonely, they might act impulsively and seek out romantic experiences that can lead to short-lived affairs.

Emotions are heightened during the full moon, making it hard for them to relax. Listening to music can help calm them down. Leo moons can experience enhanced creativity and a heightened need to express themselves during a full moon. They should focus their energy on getting in touch with their inner feelings and desires. Withdrawing and spending time alone can help with self-reflection.

FINDING PASSION

Leo moons are passionate and energetic people. Making others happy fulfills them. They crave love and develop deep bonds and emotional connections with people in their personal and professional lives. Their greatest passion comes through romantic relationships and intimacy. Being in love helps them feel a sense of purpose and gives them something to look forward to. Passion, sexuality, and attraction are important in relationships. Boredom kills Leo moon's passion and loving feelings. Excitement, variety, and spontaneity keep their emotional juices flowing. Leo moons can be perceived as self-centered, selfish lovers. They want what they want and have difficulty compromising once they make up their mind.

Being recognized for their creativity, talent, leadership ability, and sense of humor motivates them. Leo moons need to feel important and respected. Natural-born leaders, they want to share ideas and feel listened to. They feel the need to stand out from others and be seen as special. Receiving applause, praise, and attention motivates them.

Participating in sports or hobbies soothes their soul. Being a part of a team or group motivates Leo moons to produce. Goals inspire them to do better, work harder, and succeed. They have a competitive spirit and want to be the best at everything they do. If someone is more talented than they are, Leo moons will want to connect with them. Leo moons will work tirelessly to win. They see life as a stage—a competition—and they strive for accolades. Being seen, known, respected, and admired is what makes them feel alive.

Leo moon people thrive when they can openly express their feelings. Affection, sexual chemistry, and physical touch are important to Leo moons. Cuddling, holding hands, tickling, and wrestling with loved ones are playful ways they show love. They enjoy writing, teaching, and acting because they're fun and uplift others' lives.

FINDING EMOTIONAL FULFILLMENT

Leo moons feel emotionally fulfilled when they are in charge; their confidence is bolstered when all eyes are on them. Having the authority to make decisions fulfills them. They want others to look up to them and respect their position; this increases their self-esteem. Being liked, valued, and respected by others brings emotional fulfillment. It's difficult for them to be disliked.

Friendly, caring, and sociable, Leo moons will try to charm their enemies in an attempt to win them over. Deep down, they want everyone to like them; they need to feel special.

Finding loyal friends and partners is key to their emotional fulfillment. Their happiness is tied to the happiness of those closest to them. Experiencing love and expressing their heartfelt feelings brings fulfillment. They don't like being alone and need people around them to talk to and share ideas with. They may move from one relationship to the next to avoid feelings of loneliness.

Being part of a group that shares a similar mission and purpose is rewarding. Teaching and public speaking can bring fulfillment. Leo moons are generous and enjoy giving and receiving gifts. Sharing kindness and love with the world brings contentment.

LEO MOON COMFORT

Leo moons surround themselves with positive people and beautiful environments. Their home is their castle, and like a king or queen, their emotional stability depends on their home being safe and comfortable. Having gorgeous paintings, statues, and decorations in their home brings comfort. Leo moons like to own nice things, and they work hard to achieve their goals in order to acquire the comforts that they desire. They are known to live a life of luxury. Having money brings comfort because it enables them to purchase whatever they desire.

Leo moons feel inspired when they can take risks, so they grow restless if things are too relaxed. Their greatest comfort comes from competition, winning, and challenging themselves to reach their dreams. Living life to the fullest, taking risks, and experiencing newness helps reduce boredom. They feel the most comfortable when they are able to express their lighthearted, fun-loving, and easygoing personality.

Leo moon's comfort is also connected to other people. They need to feel cherished by loved ones. Not only do they need to feel loved and supported, they also require the space and freedom to be themselves. Leo moons expect partners to make them a priority. Exploring and having fun in a relationship are musts. They might not be very comfortable in committed relationships, but Leo moons are exciting, adventurous, romantic partners.

LEO MOON HAPPINESS

Leo moons exude happiness and are genuinely positive people. It takes a lot to impact their sunny nature. Naturally energetic, they like to be on the go at all times. They are happiest when they are part of a group. They need social networks and to be surrounded by people who can provide emotional support; they dislike being alone. Emotional happiness comes easily for Leo moons as long as they feel loved; being accepted for who they are and having friends who make them feel special inspires them.

Romance, passion, and intimacy are critical for Leo moons to find true happiness. Love affairs can bring happiness, but Leo moons often avoid long-term commitments. When they do fall in love, it motivates them to conquer any challenge. Making their loved ones laugh brings Leo moons joy.

Being grateful helps Leo moons attract what they want. However, they naturally experience good luck because of their positive outlook on life. They have the ability to see silver linings in even the most difficult situations.

Leo moons express their emotions through communication, writing, acting, or creating something special. Being financially stable enough to pursue expensive hobbies, artistic interests, and creative pursuits heightens feelings of happiness. Attending concerts, traveling, and gambling can be exciting outlets to explore.

Leo moons are children at heart, so being playful makes them happy. They enjoy mentoring, motivating, and inspiring creativity in those around them.

LEO MOON TRANSFORMATION

Leo moons transform when they stop caring about what other people think of them. Being self-absorbed and expecting to be loved can prevent growth. Leo moons need to realize they are special regardless of what others say. They benefit when they overcome insecurities and develop greater confidence.

Creating positive relationships with others helps them feel less lonely. Leo moons tend to dominate relationships and express strong emotions. Sometimes family and friends feel controlled and ignored. Other people might not take time to get to know them based on first impressions. Displays of confidence can be perceived as arrogance. Leo moons often think about their own feelings first; having their needs met is their top priority.

Leo moon people can be quite stubborn and focused on their own ideas. When they feel something strongly, they experience difficulty changing direction. Even when they know they should let people who are more knowledgeable guide them, there is an inner resistance. Leo moons need to transform their need to always be right and listen to other people's advice instead. Appreciating the wisdom of those who have more experience than they do is the first step toward transforming this trait.

Leo moons care about what other people think about them and appreciate constructive feedback. Direct, honest, and kind people melt their hearts. They will try their best to change their behavior if they know it is upsetting someone.

If Leo moons didn't have a supportive home life, forgiving their parents, siblings, or family members for wrongdoing helps them develop courage. Transformation comes when they learn to love and value their own emotions.

LEO MOON HEALING

Leo moons are known to brag and highlight their own achievements. They do this when they feel insecure or aren't getting adequate attention. Flattery and kind words are what Leo moons crave most from others. If people in their lives are unable to do this, they feel hurt and ignored. Their need for praise pushes people away and can cause tension in relationships. Status and power should not be the focus of their life—they heal when they shift their focus onto finding an inner sense of satisfaction.

Leo moon's relationships often suffer because friends, family, and coworkers feel they aren't listened to. They can make others feel inferior when they refuse to acknowledge other people's ideas have value. Letting others be recognized and making an extra effort to give other people credit will create healthier relationships. Leo moons heal when they learn to be humbler. Acknowledging mistakes and admitting when they are wrong will help heal relationships.

Healing comes from within, but Leo moons often seek healing outside themselves, from other people. Receiving validation and support feels healing because, deep down, they want to please others. Leo moon people heal when they learn to love themselves and stop trying to get attention from others. They spend a lot of time trying to win and compete in order to prove themselves, but they work hard for what they want and still feel emotionally empty in the end. They heal when they give emotional attention to themselves regardless of how others treat them. Valuing themselves is the most healing thing they can do.

Laughing and joking around can also be healing. Being easygoing and lighthearted will help Leo moons through many difficult times.

LEO MOON RESILIENCY

Resilience comes easily for Leo moons because of their optimism, positivity, and happy-go-lucky attitude. They naturally focus on the bright side. When bad things do happen, they possess a powerful ability to adapt to crisis. They quickly overcome challenges because of their determination and emotional strength. Leo moons don't give up easily and like to be seen as a leader.

Writing and talking about their problems helps Leo moon people through difficult times. They don't like repressing their feelings—they want to share them with the world. Socially adept, they have an ability to find others who support them. When they have a strong circle of trusted friends, Leo moons feel they can overcome anything life throws their way. Finding true love, romance, and passion also inspires Leo moons to move forward from difficult life situations.

More than anything, Leo moons want to feel like they belong. They feel best when they are a part of something larger than themselves. Being part of a team makes them stronger. Feeling like they are making an impact and sharing a common goal with a group helps them develop greater resilience.

LEO MOON VALUES

Leo moon people like to be in charge and don't like taking orders from others; they want to make decisions on their own. Doing what they want to do and being able to act on their feelings in the moment is important to them because Leo moons value having freedom and independence.

Career progression is more valuable to Leo moons than money or possessions. They want to hold a prestigious position of authority at a high level; reaching the top is important to them because it's tied to their self-esteem. They work hard but expect others to notice and compliment them for their efforts. Leo moon people need to receive formal recognition for their accomplishments: awards, certificates, pay increases, and public praise are all things they strive for. A good compliment is the quickest way to a Leo moon's heart. They want to feel respected, acknowledged, and appreciated.

Leo moons surround themselves with successful, talented, and important people. They know who to make friends with at work and who can help them on their career path—they're always seeking out those who can benefit them in some way. Being self-assured and expressive helps Leo moons develop social connections easily; they are networkers and woo people with their outgoing nature. They focus on developing friendships with people they admire and are able to rise up the ranks quite easily due to their charm, charisma, and powerful connections.

Leo moons value powerful, intelligent, creative people and those who stand out from the crowd. They are attracted to people with special gifts, like athletes, artists, musicians, and actors. This is because Leo moons value specialness in themselves *and* others.

Leo moons value relationships and attention almost as much as they value recognition. Showering others with love and affection is a natural gift, and receiving love in return can be rewarding.

At the end of the day, Leo moons like to let their hair down and pursue activities that give them an adrenaline rush. They are playful and like to have fun. Attending sporting events, concerts, and parties is important to them. Chasing excitement and adventure helps Leo moons attain their main goal: to enjoy life.

LEO MOON SELF-CARE

Self-care for Leo moons should involve some type of social activity, physical movement, and challenge. Traveling, exploring the outdoors, and networking are ways they can unwind.

Getting out of the house with friends and doing something fun helps Leo moons forget about their problems. They feel relaxed when they are supported and surrounded by people. Hosting parties, eating out, attending social gatherings, and going to sporting events can be beneficial. Competing in sports, playing games, taking risks, and gambling are ways to get their mind off their troubles.

Leo moons might withdraw and prefer being alone when they are depressed. They don't want anyone close to them to see them sad. Avoiding others when they don't feel good is how they practice self-care. This won't last long, though, because they feel their best when they are around other people.

LEO MOON SELF-CARE PROMPTS

Tapping into their creativity helps Leo moons express their inner feelings. Painting or drawing, writing poetry, and journaling encourage reflection.

1. Where do you find passion?

2. What makes you happy?

3. What moon sign traits make you resilient?

4. What artistic or creative gifts do you possess?

5. What makes you feel comfortable?

6. How do you handle emotional stress?

7. What is something positive you learned from your mother?

8. What self-care tips are you going to implement?

9. List three things that bring you emotional fulfillment.

10. List three things that you are grateful for.

LEO MOON AFFIRMATIONS

- "I share the limelight."

- "I love others deeply, and that is one of my greatest strengths."

- "I value myself and don't need the approval of others."

- "My hobbies are important and I always make time for them."

- "Expressing my creative side helps me heal."

CHAPTER

Moon in Virgo

Nickname: Virgo the Servant

Symbol: The maiden

Sun Sign Dates: August 23–September 22

Ruler: Mercury

Rules: The sixth house; the digestive system

Sign Type: Earth, mutable

Polar Opposite Sign: Pisces

Keyword: "I analyze"

Tips for Healing: Prioritize self-care, make time to relax, feel your emotions

Key Traits: Intellectual, perfectionistic, responsible, efficient, critical, helpful, high-strung

Values: Routine, neatness, efficiency, knowledge, competence, service to others

Maslow's Hierarchy of Needs: Physical and security needs

Virgo is ruled by the earth element. Grounded, practical, and detail oriented, Virgo moons like order and efficiency. As a mutable sign, they are flexible and open-minded; if needed, they can change and adapt to situations.

Virgo moons are perfectionists who have a keen eye for detail. They are perceptive and highly observant, so they notice things that most people don't. With their laser-like vision, they see through clutter and confusion to fix things that are not working. Working toward perfection makes them happy, but these tendencies can also make it difficult for them to relax. Virgo moons often feel unsteady if they have to work in a disorganized environment. They like their home and office space to be neat and tidy. Making to-do lists, grocery lists, and organizing things helps them feel emotionally secure. Practical things bring stability, order, and happiness into their lives.

Virgo moons are polite, tactful, shy, and refined, but they're also deeply self-conscious. Because Virgo moons are self-aware, they recognize their own faults and weaknesses. They work hard to change anything about themselves that they feel is negative, and they are internally motivated to become a better person.

When it comes to emotions, Virgo moons can feel uncomfortable; they prefer to keep their feelings to themselves. Conscientious, shy, and private, they see emotions as unstable and illogical. As a result, repressing and restricting emotions is common for this moon sign. Because they are naturally laser-focused, Virgo moons believe they can think of a practical solution to every problem. But Virgo moon people need to realize that some things can't be figured out, and thinking can't always solve emotional problems. If left unchecked, this tendency can lead to obsessing over irrelevant details.

An overactive mind creates anxiety. Virgo moon people are worriers and fret over small things. When they calm their mind, their emotions become more balanced. To do this, Virgo moons should pace themselves and make time for relaxation, meditation, and solitude. Being alone is helpful when they experience stress and anxiety. Recharging their emotional battery is critical in order for them to truly be able to help others.

Helping others is Virgo moon's natural gift, and they need to be making a difference in some way to feel satisfied. Service-oriented and self-sacrificing, they can be found volunteering at homeless shelters, working with abused animals, or caring for children. They have a deep emotional need to relieve other people's pain. They make excellent psychologists and social workers because they offer practical advice to those who are struggling, and they notice small details about patterns of behavior. Burnout, emotional depletion, and fatigue can impact their lives because they are always giving to others. Selflessness is second nature, but Virgo moons need to learn how to say no. It is important for them to develop strong boundaries. If they don't, people may take advantage of their kindness and willingness to help.

One of the most challenging things for a Virgo moon is going with the flow. They like to control things, fix things, organize, and plan each step. Routine, structure, and stability are important to them, both in their personal and professional lives. When allowed to work at their own pace, Virgo moons are dedicated, productive employees. They are blessed with the ability to multitask and can accomplish a great deal of projects. However, Virgo moon people prefer working alone. They get more done when they are able to have private space. When they get distracted from their work, they get frustrated and can lash out verbally.

Natural workhorses, Virgo moon people have a hard time slowing down and relaxing until everything is completed. Work is very important for their emotional satisfaction. They can push through many tasks on pure adrenaline, but sometimes they push themselves too far. Burnout happens if they neglect their own needs. Hardworking and dedicated, they need to find work-life harmony. Virgo moons should avoid neglecting their personal life for work; their work will always be there, and their health, family, and friends also need their attention.

Virgo moon people have a stable energy that makes them excellent friends. They will do anything for those they love. They naturally take care of everyone's needs quietly, modestly, and dutifully. They avoid emotional drama and entanglements. And, because they are super responsible, they hate letting anyone down. Virgo moons make excellent spouses and are supportive, reliable, and helpful around the house. Traditional at heart, they enjoy owning their own home, having a pet, being married, and raising children. They need a secure home life in order to go out into the world to achieve their goals; if their home is disruptive, they struggle to find a stable routine.

Relationships can be challenging for Virgo moons. They are known to dislike public displays of affection or showing any emotional vulnerability. Sometimes they may appear cold or unloving. The truth is they show their love by doing practical things for their partner. Cleanliness is important in many areas of their lives, and in similar fashion, they don't like emotional drama. They prefer stability, practicality, and duty in intimate relationships. Clear communication with someone who inspires them is attractive to a Virgo moon; it takes a special person to ignite their inner passion. To feel love, Virgo moons need a mental connection. They often attract partners with a completely opposite emotional nature.

I know several Virgo moons, and we get along wonderfully because I'm a sun sign Virgo. One friend of mine is a perfectionist and has high expectations. She has natural writing gifts and is able to pinpoint any spelling error or flaw in a document. I value her input and ability to tell me the truth. Virgo moons make supportive coworkers, family, and friends. They want to make things better for everyone and genuinely care about others. Other people might perceive Virgo moons as controlling, bossy, or critical, but they are just trying to help because they care.

Virgo moon people are eloquent and express themselves well. Giving advice comes naturally to them, but they have difficulty truly listening to others. They need to work on paying attention to what others say. In their mind, they're always planning their verbal response, and this distracts them from the essence of what is being communicated. They like to help their loved ones solve problems and analyze the situation to find solutions. Service-oriented at heart, Virgo moons want to help others and alleviate the suffering of those around them. Many are drawn to the helping professions because they have a strong desire to make a difference in people's lives.

Virgo moon people have a fast, quick mind that absorbs information easily. Having many different hobbies and interests is necessary to prevent feelings of stagnation. They are excellent communicators; explaining complex subjects in an easy-to-understand way is a talent, which makes them fantastic teachers. They have a gift for analyzing things on a deeper level. Highly intelligent, they make excellent students. Teaching, writing, editing, and learning are important to them.

If a Virgo moon had a mother figure present in their life, she might have had these traits, as the moon rules the mother. Virgo moon's mother figure was task oriented, conscientious, perfectionistic, critical, and health conscious. She was probably overprotective and made sure that everyone took their vitamins and ate healthy food. She was perceived as intelligent, kind, and talkative; education and learning were a priority in the home. Clear communication was a big part of Virgo moon's childhood, and their social skills were learned from their mother. High standards and perfectionistic tendencies were passed down. The mother was often at work, constantly busy achieving something. She was sometimes high-strung and found it difficult to relax.

HOW THE FULL MOON AFFECTS VIRGO MOON

When the moon is full, Virgo moon people feel unsettled and more restless. It may be difficult for them to quiet their active mind. Overthinking is intensified during this time, as is overanalyzing. Enhanced anxiety and obsessive thoughts can make it difficult to relax. They can experience difficulty sleeping. Their anxiety level increases during the full moon, and they will feel more restless.

Virgo moons may feel more vulnerable and irritable during a full moon. They are forced to feel their emotions as they bubble up to the surface. Being practical and grounded is a major part of their personality, but during a full moon they will feel their inhibitions lower. Virgo moons might say and do things they normally would not do. Irritability and criticalness can impact relationships, causing conflict. Typically shy and reserved, they may feel emotionally unsettled during a full moon.

FINDING PASSION

Virgo moons are passionate about serving others and helping those in need. They enjoy making other people's lives better. They are drawn to healing professions such as nursing, alternative medicine, veterinary work, counseling, social work, and childcare. Inner motivation comes through being of service. Virgo moons are passionate about making things perfect. They have high standards for themselves and others. Expectations push them to find what is meaningful and pursue it. Feeling appreciated is key—they will continue to serve if they feel it is helping others.

Virgo moons are passionate communicators and highly intelligent. Sharing ideas, thoughts, and goals with others helps them connect. Finding a reliable partner to love opens them up to passionate feelings they did not know they had. Virgo moons are usually uncomfortable with feeling emotions, so when they feel love for someone, it scares them. They often overanalyze and pick apart their feelings. This personality trait is a way they maintain feelings of stability and a sense of control over their life. They are passionate about finding loyal friends and people who they can open up to on a deeper level—it just takes Virgo moons a little more time to trust others with their inner world.

Having a successful career where they can help others brings passion into their life. Virgo moon people like to be productive and see results, and they are efficient, detail oriented, and blessed with a surplus of energy to complete tasks. Being recognized for their work and given additional duties inspires them. Reaching their goals gives them a strong desire to do even more. Virgo moon people experience passion when they feel needed and appreciated. Virgo moons are passionate about working, learning, and organizing things.

Taking classes, reading, pursuing hobbies, and mastering new skills motivates Virgo moons. They are passionate about learning new things and obtaining knowledge. Bettering themselves is a lifelong mission, and Virgo moon people make an effort to become more self-aware. They always strive for perfection; eliminating unwanted behaviors, thoughts, and beliefs is a way they pursue growth.

FINDING EMOTIONAL FULFILLMENT

Mastering tasks and doing everything correctly brings Virgo moons emotional fulfillment. It can be challenging for Virgo moons to feel content because they have high standards for themselves and others; striving to do everything perfectly can be a heavy burden. Accepting the fact that they are human and allowed to make mistakes helps them relax. They need to realize no one is perfect and be gentler with themselves. Self-love is beneficial.

Relationships can be challenging for Virgo moons. They want to trust and be able to depend on others, but this takes time. Finding a responsible, dedicated partner is their goal. The problem is they tend to be judgmental, and others become convinced they will never be happy. Unfortunately, Virgo moons see people's faults—and they glaringly stand out. This can lead Virgo moons to be critical of loved ones, but they do this because they are trying to help. Learning to accept people for who they are instead of trying to change them will help create healthier and happier relationships.

Fulfillment comes from having a solid routine and knowing what to expect. Change and uncertainty cause additional stress and worry. The more they can control the outcome of situations, the more fulfilled they will be. Worry kicks in when they feel overwhelmed. Order, structure, and planning things bring fulfillment. When their lives are stable, secure, and organized, they are capable of achieving great things and can easily move past difficulties.

When Virgo moons are working toward a goal—such as taking care of family members, children, or other people—they experience fulfillment.

VIRGO MOON COMFORT

Virgo moons are most comfortable when their world is clean, organized, and structured. They like knowing what to expect! They enjoy being cozy at home, surrounded by their pets, family, and friends. Reading, writing, studying, and watching educational documentaries are soothing. Accumulating ideas and knowledge helps them connect to things that are important to them.

Curling up on the couch, reading a good book, or writing are things that bring comfort and relieve anxiety. Cooking, cleaning, rearranging, and organizing things makes Virgo moons feel better. It is hard for them to relax at home if things are messy, cluttered, or scattered.

Analyzing things, overthinking, and obsessing over small details can make Virgo moon people feel off-balance. When that happens, they need to withdraw and balance their energy. Solitude is crucial for Virgo moon's well-being. Getting in touch with their restless thoughts and processing them helps them unwind. Thinking through obstacles is relaxing, and they enjoy making to-do lists. Being prepared brings comfort and gives Virgo moons the strength to overcome difficulties.

Accomplishing practical tasks and working hard bring emotional comfort. Getting things done and off their plate makes them feel better. Virgo moons should make to-do lists and focus on prioritizing things that are important to them. They tend to take on a lot of responsibilities at home, with family, and at work. Adequate expectations and learning how to say no are things Virgo moons would benefit from. Being efficient and focusing on small details makes them feel useful, but they should not neglect their own health and life. Self-sacrificing behaviors will negatively impact them.

VIRGO MOON HAPPINESS

Virgo moons are happiest when they are helping other people. Doing practical things for people they care about is top priority. As a service-oriented moon sign, they want to keep busy. Being productive, checking things off their to-do list, and finishing tasks makes them feel good. Taking care of people and animals makes them happy. Many adopt and rescue neglected animals. Since Virgo moons feel inspired to help animals in some way, they may enjoy volunteering at animal shelters. Some Virgo moon people are drawn to veterinarian work.

Caring for family members who are sick or helping a coworker complete a task makes them feel happy. They enjoy feeling needed by others. Because Virgo moons do not communicate emotions easily, they prefer doing acts of service to show their love. Virgo moon people find happiness by staying active and serving others in some way.

Virgo moons dislike surprises, instability, and crisis situations. They feel content when they have a balanced routine and know what to expect. Monotony makes them happy; they enjoy repetitive tasks and mastering skills. Change is difficult for them, but they have to learn to adapt to the unknown. Resisting change will disrupt their happiness.

VIRGO MOON TRANSFORMATION

Virgo moons transform when they realize that being perfect isn't realistic and it's okay to make mistakes. Learning not to be hard on themselves helps them overcome difficult emotional experiences. They have high standards and expectations that are hard to live up to.

Conquering worry and obsessive thoughts will help Virgo moon people feel more positive about life. Overcoming a need to control the outcome of a situation helps them transform. If Virgo moons learn to let go and trust the Universe to provide what they need, they will become stronger. Developing faith and letting go of things they can't control transforms their outlook on life. They would benefit from transforming pessimistic thoughts and embracing a more positive outlook.

Virgo moons are self-sacrificing and give a lot of their time and energy to others. They transform when they stop neglecting their own emotional needs. Learning how to relax and taking better care of their health by eating right, getting enough sleep, exercising, and taking time away from work helps them overcome burnout. Overachievers and workaholics, Virgo moons transform when they make their personal lives more of a focus. Working hard comes naturally, but they have to balance their personal and work life.

Shyness can prevent Virgo moons from developing deeper relationships. They benefit from stepping out of their comfort zone and talking to people first. Making the first move can be scary, but they grow in self-confidence when they take risks.

Once Virgo moons feel comfortable, they are excellent communicators, but it takes them a while to trust others. Embracing vulnerability and developing intimate relationships helps them transform into a more trusting person. It takes a special person to pull them out of their introverted shell, but once they connect with someone, they are extremely devoted partners. Virgo moon people change who they are when they experience sex and intimacy; they feel more confident when they find someone to love.

VIRGO MOON HEALING

Virgo moons are excellent at healing other people and are able to alleviate others' emotional pain. Natural counselors and communicators, they offer wonderful advice to those in need and have a calm, healing presence. Taking care of others helps them heal their own inner wounds.

Virgo moons are always working hard and setting goals. Just like worker bees, they can accomplish a great deal. They succeed in the helping professions because they are highly committed, passionate, and energetic about work. Balancing their practical and emotional needs will help them be healthier. They heal when they find time to relax, take a vacation, and spend quality time with their family.

Releasing high standards and expectations helps Virgo moons heal insecurities. They can be very hard on themselves when they fall short of living up to their high standards, and giving themselves grace helps them heal unpleasant emotions. Virgo moons heal emotional wounds when they learn to focus on their feelings. Accepting positive *and* negative emotions also helps them find contentment.

Virgo moons heal when they learn how to implement self-care activities into their lives. Establishing a sleep routine, prioritizing a healthy diet, and making time for fun will help them heal. They're so focused on helping others and accomplishing tasks that they do not take good care of themselves. In order to continue to help others heal, they need to fill up their own cup first. Learning to control their active mind and express their thoughts is important. Spending time outdoors and getting fresh air helps them recharge, as does spending time alone, writing, journaling, and practicing self-reflection. Seeking out alternative medicine techniques such as Reiki energy healing, yoga, Bach flower remedies, herbology, and acupuncture can help heal ailments that traditional medicine can't resolve. They might also benefit from utilizing these skills in their professional life.

VIRGO MOON RESILIENCY

Virgo moons develop strength when they overcome obsessive thoughts. Their mind affects their mood more than other signs, so it's important for them to control negative thinking. They tend to worry, obsess, and overanalyze things to the point of exhaustion. Routines and planning help them feel in control of their environment, and they feel off-balance, anxious, and stressed when faced with unexpected situations. Once Virgo moons learn to change their perspective and focus on what they are grateful for, they adapt easily.

Working hard and accomplishing tasks comes easily for them, and staying busy helps them keep their mind off their problems. But this can become a way that Virgo moons avoid feeling their emotions. They struggle when they have to feel intense emotions, and they use logic to try to figure out why they feel a certain way. Their practical personality traits help Virgo moons overcome loss and grief; they know feelings are changeable and try not to get too wrapped up in their emotions. Keeping busy helps them remain resilient. Their selfless nature gives them strength to adapt to many challenges.

Virgo moons look at things from a practical point of view and don't let emotions guide their decisions. Being realistic helps Virgo moons work through their problems. Their sarcastic sense of humor can also alleviate emotionally heavy situations. These traits help them overcome obstacles and develop greater resilience.

VIRGO MOON VALUES

Virgo moon people value a stable routine. They like to organize their world and prepare for each day, so instability creates worry. Their daily routine needs to be consistent, and they should have a set plan on when they go to bed at night, when they wake up, when they eat breakfast, what time they exercise, when they walk their dog, and when they leave for work. Virgo moons value predictability and appreciate things being organized.

A clean environment is crucial. Virgo moon people might find it difficult to relax if things are cluttered. They have high standards for cleanliness regarding their physical body and environment. There is usually one area of their life where they have to have things organized just so; it might be their office, car, bedroom, bathroom, or kitchen. They may experience obsessive-compulsive tendencies, and repetition makes them feel better. Virgo moons value others who respect their need for organization and cleanliness.

A chaotic environment will be unsettling for Virgo moons. They will find it difficult to cope emotionally and have trouble focusing on completing tasks. This is detrimental because Virgo moons value hard work and efficiency. Producing results quickly is important to them because they do not like making unnecessary effort. Stability, comfort, and security are valuable to them.

Virgo moons want excellence in all that they do. Perfectionists at heart, they strive to do everything correctly and go above and beyond to make sure every error is caught before they turn something in. Achievement comes easily for them due to their ability to impress their superiors.

Helping others is their forte, and coworkers will value their generous nature. Virgo moon people want to use what they know to make the world a better place. Alleviating other people's struggles by providing support makes them feel useful. Taking care of others is what they do best, and it gives them a sense of purpose. Volunteering and community service are things they value. Making a positive impact on other people's lives and leaving a legacy behind are important to Virgo moons.

Virgo moons also value learning and knowledge. They are intelligent and like to read, take classes, and master difficult subjects. They learn through experience, and they are subject matter experts in whatever they do. They value competence because it's a practical skill that is action oriented.

VIRGO MOON SELF-CARE

Virgo moon people are often high-strung and have trouble quieting their active mind, so they benefit from self-care activities that help them control their thoughts. Being in the present moment is important. Stretching, yoga, meditation, cooking, cleaning, and organizing their home are relaxing. Reading is another great activity. Any activity that helps Virgo moons shut off their thoughts helps them find balance.

Always focused on helping other people, Virgo moons are known to neglect their own needs. They need time to recharge. Solitude helps them feel grounded. Listening to music, enjoying peaceful surroundings, and sitting in silence are beneficial self-care tools. Spending time outdoors in nature, walking, and hiking rejuvenates them. Writing and journaling can help them release stress.

VIRGO MOON SELF-CARE PROMPTS

Expressing emotions is easier for Virgo moons when they write things down.

1. Where do you find passion?

2. What makes you happy?

3. What moon sign traits make you resilient?

4. How do you balance your work and home life?

5. What makes you feel comfortable?

6. How do you handle emotional stress?

7. What is something positive you learned from your mother?

8. What self-care tips are you going to implement?

9. List three things that bring you emotional fulfillment.

10. List three things you are grateful for.

VIRGO MOON AFFIRMATIONS

- "I feel and express my emotions."

- "I take care of myself by making time for self-care."

- "I trust the Universe."

- "I balance my work and personal life."

- "I release the need to control things."

MOON IN LIBRA

Nickname: Libra the Peacemaker

Symbol: The scales

Sun Sign Dates: September 23–October 23

Ruler: Venus

Rules: The seventh house; the kidneys and lower back

Sign Type: Air, cardinal

Polar Opposite Sign: Aries

Keyword: "I balance"

Tips for Healing: Make tough decisions, find balance, prioritize relationships

Key Traits: Diplomatic, fair, artistic, creative, adaptable, indecisive, dependent

Values: Peace, harmony, fairness, balance, knowledge, partnership, marriage, beauty

Maslow's Hierarchy of Needs: Social and security needs

Libra is ruled by the air element. Libra moons possess both intellectual and artistic talents and like socializing. As a cardinal sign, they have many new and creative ideas they want to share with others.

Libra moons are talented at art, music, design, education, and intellectual pursuits. Many are good at math and science. They like to learn and are extremely intelligent people, which is common for air signs. Libra moon people need both mental and emotional outlets in order to express their inner nature. Ultimately, they need a way to express their creative abilities because they find true happiness in artistic and creative pursuits.

Going with the flow and adapting to situations comes easily for them. This is because Libra moons need peace and harmony in their lives and avoid conflict-ridden situations. Stress builds up if they have to make decisions because they dislike having to choose. Talented at always seeing both sides of an issue, they avoid committing to a certain path. This is largely because pleasing others is their priority, and Libra moons worry they will upset others if they disagree with them. They avoid conflict and can passively withdraw when they feel tension. Facing conflict is the most difficult thing for Libra moons, but they need to learn how to speak up about what they think and feel. Reluctance and hesitancy to act cause problems if Libra moons refuse to address issues head-on.

Libra moons value compromise, fairness, justice, and beauty. When they see inequality in the world, it bothers them; Libra moons can often be heard saying, "That is not right." Fighting for the underdog is something they are passionate about. They often find it hard to choose a career path because they are interested in many different things, but because they believe everything should be fair, Libra moon people are attracted to careers where they can fight for victims of crime and maintain justice. Usually, Libra moons find themselves working in law enforcement of some kind. Excellent at seeing both sides of any issue, they are born diplomats, mediators, and problem solvers. Giving advice to others and helping other people resolve problems comes easily to them and makes them feel useful.

Libra moons are always trying to find balance; loved ones can help them maintain equilibrium. Charming and funny, it's easy for Libra moons to make friends. They need to be surrounded by people who inspire and support their dreams. Socializing and spending quality time with people they care about is important for their mental health. Companionship is critical for Libra moon's happiness; without it, they will feel isolated and lonely. Other people help keep them centered and grounded, especially during stressful times.

Illusive and sometimes difficult to understand, Libra moons don't always share their feelings with others. They can appear distant, aloof, and emotionally detached. In addition, Libra moons act like nothing bothers them (it takes a lot to rattle them or make them angry). Some think they are too easygoing, but many people appreciate their demureness and calming presence. Others are attracted to their natural beauty and social grace. Sophisticated, elegant, and often introverted, other people are always trying to figure out what Libra moons are thinking.

Relationships help Libra moons feel balanced and supported, so finding love is important. When they find someone they like, it is not uncommon for Libra moons to push them away. This is because they are indecisive and fear intimacy. Their emotions swing back and forth, and this confuses people close to them. They might be involved in many relationships before they find their lifelong partner. Libra moons dislike being alone and find out more about themselves through their partner. Opposites attract, and people who are different from them can create a balance in their lives. Dependable and affectionate partners are a good match for Libra moons. Soul mate relationships are common because Libra moons are on a search for true love and won't settle for anything less.

Communication in relationships can be challenging because of Libra moon's need to please others. Sacrificing their own thoughts and feelings for their partner eventually causes problems. There is no way to avoid conflict 100 percent of the time; arguments will eventually impact their relationships. Libra moons need to stop being people pleasers and trust that the right people will stay in their lives. They are meant to learn how to develop boundaries in relationships.

Sometimes Libra moons doubt their emotions and can become moody. Always swaying back and forth, trying to make up their mind, causes confusion. When this happens, they isolate themselves from others, which only makes their moodiness worse. When they feel alone, Libra moons need to make extra effort to reach out to friends, send text messages, or make phone calls. Sometimes they wait for others to reach out to them, but Libra moon people feel best when they reach out first. Being more direct and sharing their feelings are major lessons to learn.

If Libra moons had a mother figure present in their life, she might have had these traits, as the moon represents the mother in the birth chart. The mother figure was artistic, attractive, intelligent, and peaceful. She was perceived as calm, kind, and soft-spoken. Art, music, and education were important topics that

Libra moons were encouraged to learn. As a child, they observed their mother needing support from other people. The relationship the mother had with her partner taught Libra moons a lot about commitment. Some Libra moons believed their mother was codependent and indecisive and would not speak up for herself. Conflict was an issue in the home, or the mother protected Libra moons from ever witnessing anger, conflict, disagreements, or unpleasant emotions.

HOW THE FULL MOON AFFECTS LIBRA MOON

Libra moons feel more irritable during a full moon. They experience increased emotions, which makes them uncomfortable. Fluctuations of mood and indecisiveness might increase during this time. Because they will feel unbalanced, they'll withdraw to try to maintain a sense of stability. This need for solitude and alone time is not typical for them.

Relationships can be more challenging for Libra moons during the full moon due to irritability and conflict. If they have been avoiding speaking up about something that has been bothering them, this is the time they verbalize it. This catches their family, friends, and loved ones off guard because Libra moons are typically agreeable and peaceful. This is a good time to clear the air of any unpleasant emotions.

If they are able to focus their energy, creative ideas and artistic energy are heightened during this time. Libra moons should paint, draw, write, or create something beautiful during the full moon. Listening to music is beneficial because it decreases stress and increases positive feelings. Spending time with their partner, children, or parents can bring comfort during this restless time.

FINDING PASSION

Libra moons find their passion when they mediate conflict. Creating peaceful and harmonious relationships with others is their calling. They are passionate about fighting for what is right and are interested in justice. Libra moons are known to fight for the underdog, and they have strong opinions about how things should be.

Building relationships with people who bring peace into their lives is important for their overall well-being. They seek out connections with people who are supportive and loving. Falling in love, experiencing intimacy, and finding a loyal partner brings passion into Libra moon's life. They feel most alive when they have deep bonds with others.

Expressing their creative interests—such as painting, playing an instrument, or journaling—helps them connect to their inner passion. Libra moons should consider communicating their feelings through art, music, or theater.

FINDING EMOTIONAL FULFILLMENT

Libra moon people feel fulfilled when others agree with them and listen to their opinions. They crave tranquility more than any other moon sign. Libra moons' emotional nature is usually calm; they feel unsteady when stressed or when they experience conflict with others. They might appear detached, but inside they feel things deeply.

Relationships are important to Libra moons, and without having someone to love, they feel lonely and isolated. Many Libra moons seek relationships and dislike being single. They might date many people before they find the right partner. At times, they question whether they will ever fall in love or meet someone special. Libra moon people spend a lot of time thinking about love and companionship. Dating is not satisfying enough for them; they desire a formal commitment. They have high standards and high romantic expectations—they want to feel butterflies. Lukewarm feelings make it difficult for them to commit or be intimate with someone. Having a long-term relationship, living with their significant other, or being married improves their overall happiness. True emotional fulfillment comes when they have a committed partner to share their life with—but finding the right partner is key. Libra moons need to be cautious about rushing into marriage and make sure they take time to get to know their significant other. Relationships can be devastating for Libra moons if they end up with an abusive, toxic, or unsupportive partner.

Libra moon's emotions are affected by those around them. If people they love are struggling, it is difficult for Libra moons to feel happy. If coworkers are angry, irritated, or burned out, then they can take on those feelings. Their mood is easily impacted, so surrounding themselves with positive people is important for their emotional well-being.

Libra moons are both intellectual and emotional souls. They need to be able to express both sides of their personality. Libra moons feel fulfilled when they can successfully balance their interests, personal life, and work life.

LIBRA MOON COMFORT

Libra moons tend to overintellectualize emotions and can get stuck in their head. Feeling grounded is critical for them to feel comfortable, but they lack the ability to stabilize themselves. Feeling supported by others helps them think more clearly and find answers to emotional problems. Surrounding themselves with earth sign moons like Taurus, Virgo, and Capricorn will help them maintain balance.

Conflict, disagreements, and negative feelings cause stress. They can't concentrate when things are tense. This is because Libra moons want to make sure everyone is happy at all times; that's the only way they feel truly grounded and calm. Maintaining a sense of balance helps Libra moons feel comfortable. They dislike change and find it unsettling. If any area of life suffers a setback, they struggle to find equilibrium. They are grateful when things are running smoothly at home and at work. Libra moon's greatest challenge is adapting and utilizing their energy to get through times of discomfort and change.

Libra moon people can be picky about who they allow into their lives. They may have many acquaintances, but only a few trusted confidants. Ultimately, Libra moons want to experience intimate relationships and true love. After all, their sense of comfort is tied to receiving love and support. Their goal is to get married, so they seek out the perfect partner to spend their lives with. They seek romantic partners who are more talkative, confident, or outgoing than they are because they enjoy attending social gatherings. Their main identity is always found through someone else. They find out who they really are by being in relationships. Libra moons are charming and flirtatious when they want to be, which makes it easy for them to attract others.

LIBRA MOON HAPPINESS

Libra moons find happiness when they see justice in the world. They believe everyone should follow the rules and do things the right way. Experiencing and witnessing fairness makes them feel good. When there is a clear sense of right or wrong, and when order surrounds them, they are happiest. Learning how to compromise and meet people in the middle benefits them.

Spending time with friends, learning new things, and expressing their creative side helps them find happiness. Socializing with others who are artistic, intelligent, and easygoing brings them out of their shell and can help them snap out of sadness and depression. Surrounding themselves with positive people inspires them and helps them avoid pessimistic tendencies.

Having someone to love makes them happy. But all relationships have some conflict, and realizing that no one is perfect can help Libra moon people accept their partner's flaws. Focusing on the good things that already exist in their partner shifts negativity and increases positive emotions. Libra moons will realize that disagreements don't have to end relationships as long as both partners are invested and put effort into making things work. Reciprocal relationships are top priority for Libra moon people; giving and taking equally is important to them. They can't feel like they are giving more than their partner—there needs to be a balance of love in the relationship or they will feel unhappy. Libra moons have high standards for relationships and romantic partners; they can become disappointed when others don't live up to their expectations. Libra moons should embrace all aspects of their partner and focus on the things they are grateful for.

Libra moons need to work on getting out of their head and connecting with their heart. When they conquer indecisiveness and make hard decisions in life, they develop greater confidence in themselves. Overcoming passivity and not avoiding unpleasant emotions helps them realize that true happiness comes from communicating their thoughts and feelings. Openness is crucial for Libra moon's happiness.

LIBRA MOON TRANSFORMATION

Libra moons become anxious if they are pressured to make a decision too quickly; they need time to gather information and want to weigh all their options. Overthinking and insecurity lead to procrastination. If they learn to trust their inner feelings, they can transform.

Balancing thoughts and feelings can be challenging for Libra moons. Many Libra moons hold back from sharing what they really think or feel due to insecurity. Passive traits prevent them from sharing and disrupt communication. They struggle with being assertive and have difficulty speaking up because it makes them feel uncomfortable. If they learn to stand up for themselves, they can transform many areas of their life. Conflict can make relationships stronger, and once Libra moons believe this, they will transform self-doubt.

Libra moons are natural peacemakers. Negotiating is their strength, and they are able to calm others down during a crisis. They give great advice and are often found helping others solve interpersonal problems. Sometimes they feel people take advantage of their kindness because they give in easily to what others want. Instead of always trying to keep the peace, Libra moons need to step out of their comfort zone. They are not comfortable acting alone and often hesitate, but Libra moons transform when they rely on themselves to make tough decisions.

Libra moons want people to like them and take it personally when they don't. Avoidant personality traits can impact their ability to connect deeply with others. Libra moon people transform when they reveal their innermost thoughts and feelings and learn to trust others. Being vulnerable helps them develop greater connections in their personal relationships. They learn who their true friends are by experiencing betrayal and heartache. Broken relationships and breakups make them stronger. Picking compatible partners is the most important thing a Libra moon can do; they receive good luck and blessings through their partner.

LIBRA MOON HEALING

Libra moons heal when they find a relationship and develop intimacy with someone else. But developing healthy relationship patterns is crucial in order for them to heal; Libra moons tend to attract self-centered and abusive partners. Healthy relationships are based on mutual respect, love, affection, and friendship. Healing comes when Libra moons learn that friendship and trust are more important than romantic passion. Extreme emotions fizzle and burn out, but true love lasts a lifetime. Picking the right partner is important for overall life satisfaction. Libra moons need true love, and when they find it, they heal all the wounds of their past.

Sometimes Libra moons focus too much energy on their partner; they might even sacrifice their own emotional needs for the ones they love. It's important to fill up their own cup first. They're always helping others solve problems and disagreements, but Libra moons heal when they focus more on their own lives. Making themselves a priority should be the goal.

Lessons are learned from embracing conflict and facing it head-on. Libra moons heal when they communicate what they really want. Compromising and discussing differing opinions in open and honest ways are important. Running away from unpleasant feelings only intensifies them. Feeling anger is a great lesson because it helps them realize they can forgive. Bad things can happen to good people, and Libra moons find solace in this truth.

LIBRA MOON RESILIENCY

Libra moons are strongest when they are surrounded by beauty and tranquility. A secure, calm, and peaceful home life helps them face difficulties.

Creating healthy relationships makes them more resilient, but jumping from one relationship to another is not healthy. They become more resilient when they spend time alone. Being single and self-reliant helps Libra moons realize they can do anything. Focusing on their own needs first helps foster independence. Libra moons need to accept that being on their own can help them grow. The moment they let go and release their need to be in a relationship is when the Universe sends them the perfect partner. Insecurities fade away and their confidence increases when they maintain an intimate relationship.

Libra moon people need to overcome an indecisive nature that prevents them from moving forward. They become more resilient when they make their own decisions. Trusting their own ideas and gut feelings helps them adapt to unexpected change. Embracing conflict helps them gain skills that foster confidence and resiliency.

Libra moon people are able to share their personal experiences with others and become a great intermediary. Compromise is their forte, and they are excellent mediators. Libra moon's strength is helping others handle disagreements.

Life is never stable, and Libra moons' emotions often sway back and forth like a seesaw. They need other people around to help ground their airy energy, but sometimes Libra moons depend too much on loved ones to fulfill their needs. Maintaining emotional balance and trusting their own inner voice helps them grow more resilient.

LIBRA MOON VALUES

Libra moon people value peaceful surroundings and harmonious relationships. Avoiding conflict and disagreements is their natural tendency. They like simplicity and avoid complicated emotional situations. Libra moons are peaceful people and function best in a stable environment. Feeling relaxed and avoiding unnecessary stress are what they value most.

They value relationships and social connections. Socializing, learning new things, having inspiring conversations, and spending time with close friends makes them feel supported. They gravitate toward optimistic, happy, and outgoing people. Libra moons want to please others, so they feel unsettled and stressed if they have to tell people they can't do something. Libra moons value maintaining a sense of balance because it helps them feel secure.

Libra moons expect fairness in life and want everyone to be treated equally. If they believe something is not right or fair, it's the one time they might speak up. They have strong opinions about how things should be done and how people should be treated. They can always see both sides of an issue and value different perspectives.

Libra moons dislike doing things solo. Partnering with others is important for their emotional well-being. Committing to another person, showing love, receiving affection, and experiencing reciprocity are all things Libra moons value. Having a strong partner who can make decisions for them takes a heavy weight off their shoulders. The fewer decisions they have to make, the better they feel. Because a committed relationship is so valuable to Libra moon people, they are known to marry early in life.

Developing business partnerships can also be valuable to Libra moons. They can learn a lot from other people's knowledge and experience. It's beneficial for Libra moon people to have a shared goal with others—perhaps a business venture—and learn to compromise. They prefer to associate with people who pursue similar values, such as intelligence, harmony, and sophistication. Libra moon people want to be a subject matter expert in whatever career field they are involved in. Education and hands-on experience help them develop greater self-confidence. Avid readers, many are self-taught on a variety of subjects and hobbies. Libra moons like to be recognized for what they know; they value knowledge and intelligence.

Libra moons admire attractive people, material things, and pleasant personalities. They like to laugh and appreciate a good sense of humor. Surrounding themselves with items that are aesthetically pleasing helps encourage them to express their artistic side.

Pursuing hobbies and balancing intellectual pursuits are equally valuable to them, but they struggle when they have to juggle too many responsibilities. Learning to be more organized will help them when they feel off-balance. Libra moons value beauty, creativity, art, and music. Playing an instrument, listening to music, reading, and learning are pursuits they value. Balancing their time between home, work, and hobbies can be stressful but is an important part of overall happiness.

LIBRA MOON SELF-CARE

Libra moons benefit from participating in self-care activities that involve focusing on their breathing. Deep breathing techniques expel toxins from the body and help reduce emotional stress, and they distract Libra moon's active mind and settle their thoughts. Mindfulness exercises can also help them feel more grounded in their physical body.

Writing, painting, taking classes, and learning new things helps them find peace. Beneficial activities include reading, playing board games, making music, and participating in activities that challenge their mind, such as word puzzles. Not having to make decisions, taking a vacation, and surrounding themselves with tranquility improves Libra moon's mood.

Quality time with partners, friends, and family is important and helps Libra moons reduce anxiety. Their home life and work environment affect Libra moon's ability to take care of their emotional needs. Finding balance in all areas of life helps Libra moons maintain adequate self-care.

LIBRA MOON SELF-CARE PROMPTS

Journaling helps Libra moons work through their unexpressed emotions.

1. Where do you find passion?

2. What makes you happy?

3. What moon sign traits make you resilient?

4. How do you handle conflict?

5. What makes you feel comfortable?

6. How do you handle emotional stress?

7. What is something positive you learned from your mother?

8. What self-care tips are you going to implement?

9. List three things that bring you emotional fulfillment.

10. List three things you are grateful for.

LIBRA MOON AFFIRMATIONS

- "I am wrong sometimes, and that is okay."

- "I am content even without a partner."

- "I express my artistic side."

- "I feel comfortable making my own decisions."

- "I face conflict and speak up when I need to."

Moon in Scorpio

Nickname: Scorpio the Secretive One

Symbol: The scorpion

Sun Sign Dates: October 24–November 21

Ruler: Pluto

Rules: The eighth house; the sexual organs and elimination system

Sign Type: Water, fixed

Polar Opposite Sign: Taurus

Keyword: "I desire"

Tips for Healing: Experience intimacy, practice forgiveness, release the past, trust others

Key Traits: Ambitious, intense, determined, secretive, jealous, controlling, emotional

Values: Loyalty, trust, authority, deep communication, money, wealth, sexual chemistry, intimacy

Maslow's Hierarchy of Needs: Social and ego needs

Scorpio moons are ruled by the water element. They experience intense emotions and have a secretive nature. As a fixed sign, they are strong-willed, dislike the unexpected, and like to be in charge. Controlling things comes naturally, and they are focused on getting what they want.

Scorpio moons are passionate, intense, and intuitive. Sometimes they get a bad rap for being cold and calculating because they look out for themselves first and are usually twenty steps ahead of others. This is because they are practical, determined, and focused on ambition. Some people are uncomfortable around them because they naturally make others feel exposed. People can be intimidated by their energy; they either attract or repel others. A Scorpio moon makes a formidable opponent. Determined, strong, and persistent, there is nothing they can't achieve if they put their heart into it. Confident and intelligent, they know how to achieve their goals.

Magnetic, sensual, and charismatic, Scorpio moons draw people into their web. Others are attracted to their energy, strength, and confidence. When they walk into a room, people notice them instantly; they possess a magnetism that is undeniable. It's easy for others to sense their emotional depth because Scorpio moons have an intense stare that pierces through others. They see all the darkness in the world and are known to be brooding.

Insightful, observant, and extremely perceptive, Scorpio moons have the ability to see through other people. They can see beneath the surface-level emotions that people portray and have a way of pulling out other people's secrets and pain. If there is something being hidden, they will uncover the truth because they are great detectives. When their spidey senses are heightened, they know there is something wrong and will figure out what it is. Perceptive, psychic, and highly intuitive, there is very little they don't notice in the environment. Because they feel people's energy, they often judge people based on their first impression, but trusting their gut instincts has never led them astray.

Scorpio moons keep things hidden and are extremely private. They hold back their true feelings in an effort to protect themselves because they do not trust others easily. It takes time for them to open up and share because they value actions over words; they want to observe people's behavior before they reveal too much of their inner self. They are good at portraying a stoic face that shows they have it all together; being vulnerable is a fear. Secretive at heart, they hide their thoughts, feelings, and plans so much that keeping secrets becomes a part of their personality. They may unconsciously hide things in order to protect themselves. Because of this, even when Scorpio moons are in relationships, they still feel alone. Past experiences of feeling betrayed make them distrust other people's motives. It takes a special person to make them feel supported, seen, and heard. As a partner they can be possessive, intensely passionate, and loyal. They expect honesty from others but can be secretive themselves. Refusing to ask for help is common because they prefer being self-reliant. Relationships can be a challenge because they often try to do things on their own without asking their partner for help.

Scorpio moon people experience extreme emotions that can be overwhelming to contain. They have a quiet, calm exterior, but simmering underneath is a boiling pot of emotions trying to bubble to the surface. Extremes are a part of their emotional nature—lukewarm feelings don't resonate with them. On the inside, they are extremely passionate; Scorpio moons feel anger, rage, jealousy, and distrust more often than other moon signs. As a result, they are serious and take things personally. Forgiving others is one of their greatest challenges. When threatened or caught off guard, they are known to push people away and emotionally withdraw. Cutting ties with people and situations is how they protect their inner emotions.

Experts at controlling their own emotions, they dislike showing any type of weakness. Making light of heavy topics helps them deal with uncomfortable emotions; they have a dark sense of humor that catches people off guard. If you confront a Scorpio moon, try to discuss something uncomfortable, or point out something they did that bothered you, they take offense. They overreact and become defensive, shutting down communication and refusing to listen. Holding grudges can destroy their relationships. This trait helps them protect themselves from future hurt, but it can lead to loneliness. Scorpio moons need to learn how to give people the benefit of the doubt. Finding and maintaining emotional balance helps them mend broken relationships.

Scorpio moon people crave a deep bond with their loved ones and need to know everything about others. They sometimes lose partners and friends due to the way they treat people; power struggles and conflict are common because of their need to feel in control. They can be possessive and overbearing, and it is hard for them to admit when they are wrong. Scorpio moons find it hard to apologize first; they wait for others to reach out and make amends. Their emotions are deep and they often repress them by avoiding talking about things.

Scorpio moon people go through extreme transformations where they feel like they have become an entirely different person overnight. It is hard for them to explain these emotional experiences to others. While these experiences can be painful, they're a part of Scorpio moon's spiritual mission to grow. Loss and grief are things Scorpio moons resonate with; they often experience death at a young age. Personal experiences with grief leave them forever changed. They understand that life is precious and things can change in the blink of an eye. Tragic life events affect the way they communicate with others but grant them a deep understanding of the cycles of life.

Scorpio moons reach their personal and professional goals through sheer determination. They make excellent psychologists, grief counselors, police officers, and detectives. Their quiet presence and ability to listen to others' problems is a gift, and solving complex emotional problems comes easily for them. Because they are practical at heart, they give realistic advice to those who seek their counsel. They have empathic abilities that can be used to help others.

Moon in Scorpio people are born with natural healing abilities, though most Scorpio moons struggle to heal their own pain. Many feel they heal by helping others; letting go of past hurt takes extra effort. They sense the future and are able to read other people's thoughts and predict their behavior. Scorpio moons often pursue some type of psychic work and can be found doing mediumship, tarot readings, aura photos, energy healing, and astrological consultations. They are drawn to the mysterious side of life, and exploring taboo subjects helps them validate their personal experiences. They are drawn to spirituality, magic, mysticism, alternative medicine, energy work such as Reiki, and new age topics like astrology and tarot. Supernatural phenomena interests them, such as ghosts, hauntings, and aliens. Some Scorpio moons hide these interests from family and friends.

In relationships, Scorpio moons experience all-or-nothing emotions; they either trust you or they don't. Intimacy and sexuality are important to them. Scorpio moons need to be careful about getting involved in unhealthy or toxic relationships. Passionate at heart, they want to connect deeply with another person. Needy or insecure partners will make them run for the hills; they prefer people who play hard to get. They need autonomy and a sense of freedom if they are in a relationship. Some Scorpio moons dislike being dependent on anyone and avoid intimate relationships. Others enjoy sexual relationships but don't want to get too close to anyone. Commitment is a serious thing for Scorpio moons, and it might take them a long time to find someone they feel is worthy of their complete attention. Many Scorpio moons marry later in life or remain single by choice. Their emotions are never lukewarm. If they love someone and have a connection, they can become obsessed with having that person in their life. On the other hand, if someone lets them down, lacks passion, betrays them, or neglects them, then they cut ties quickly and move on.

If a Scorpio moon had a mother figure present in their life, she might have had these personality traits, as the moon represents the mother. The mother figure was seen as secretive, controlling, intuitive, and independent. As a child, Scorpio moon people might have felt like they were unable to open up emotionally or share things with their mother. Feeling like their mother was hiding things from them and keeping secrets made them feel disconnected from her. On the other hand, she might have been overprotective, possessive, and overly involved in their lives. Witnessing their mother's controlling behaviors was common in childhood. At times, their mother might have lashed out at them or taken their feedback personally. She might have felt uncomfortable showing affection or emotion. Scorpio moons perceived their mother as passive-aggressive, hard to please, and overly sensitive when it came to criticism. They learned to be secretive and private because of the way their mother responded to them. Hiding things to protect themselves and internalizing feelings helped them feel in control, but issues with nurturing need to be healed.

HOW THE FULL MOON
AFFECTS SCORPIO MOON

Scorpio moons will feel a strong need to express emotions and bond with others during a full moon. This may be because they feel an increase in their energy during the full moon. Scorpio moons are typically secretive and introverted, but the full moon draws feelings to the surface. An urge to talk about their inner world increases during this time. Making time to reflect and express these feelings in healthy ways will be beneficial. Letting go and forgiving others is helpful.

Processing their inner emotions helps them avoid conflict or misunderstandings when feelings of anger, frustration, sadness, or hurt bubble up. Taking a deep breath before they speak helps them avoid hurting other people's feelings. Practicing mindfulness helps them remain calm and relaxed.

FINDING PASSION

Scorpio moons thrive in crisis situations because they feel a passion to survive. An inner fire blazes inside them when stressful things happen. They are most passionate when they are able to feel adrenaline pumping through their veins. Challenge motivates them to succeed.

Scorpio moon people are happiest when they are self-reliant and make their own decisions. They like to be in charge, controlling things and giving orders, because they like to get things done. They give all their energy to anything they commit to; they don't like giving up.

Scorpio moons are one of the most passionate moon signs because they possess a mystical and alluring energy. Sexual chemistry is important in order for them to be interested in another person; they need both physical and emotional connections in order to desire intimacy. When they find that bond, they are passionate lovers who are protective and devoted. They have high standards in relationships and are passionate about commitment. Dedicated and loyal, they thrive when they find others who feel the same.

FINDING EMOTIONAL FULFILLMENT

Scorpio moon people excel at helping others with their problems. Giving psychological advice comes naturally because they are perceptive enough to know how to guide others. Helping others also helps them heal parts of themselves.

Having a sense of control over people and their environment is fulfilling. Scorpio moons crave financial security and work hard to achieve material possessions. Money equals power and gives them the ability to live an independent lifestyle. They find emotional fulfillment through dedication and hard work.

Scorpio moons might be interested in having children or being a parent, but sometimes they have reproductive challenges. Some might have to seek help from a medical professional in order to get pregnant. Others might choose not to have children at all and enjoy focusing on their career and partner. If they do have children, they are dedicated parents who want to provide the best opportunities for their children.

Scorpio moons have the ability to strategically plan and are patient enough to wait for the right time to act. They are insightful souls who trust their intuition. They require a certain degree of independence because they need to be able to act on their gut instincts at any given moment.

Forming deep bonds with others who share personal stories, communicate their feelings, and ask for help leads to emotional fulfillment. Being able to trust others and find loyal partners means everything to them; trust and loyalty are crucial components of their intimate relationships.

SCORPIO MOON COMFORT

Scorpio moons feel most comfortable when their emotional walls are up. Being vulnerable and trusting others can be scary, especially if Scorpio moons were hurt in the past. Maintaining privacy helps them feel safe, secure, and protected. They prefer to live life behind the scenes. Avoiding situations where they won't feel exposed helps them maintain a sense of comfort. They like to observe people and assess a situation before they share their feelings; perceiving the deeper energies around them and listening to their intuition are comforting.

Scorpio moon people like to plan, strategize, and be prepared for what to expect in every situation. Planning for the future soothes them, whereas unexpected change knocks them off-balance. They like having control over their decisions, emotions, and relationships.

Having other people's trust and respect brings contentment. Sharing their wisdom with others makes them feel useful. They have lived through many emotional trials and are able to give practical advice to other people who are struggling. Comfort comes through deep intimacy and soul bonding; shallow experiences and relationships leave them feeling unfulfilled.

SCORPIO MOON HAPPINESS

Having privacy is important to Scorpio moons, but being able to share parts of themselves with someone they trust helps them feel lighter. When they are able to forgive others and let go of the past, they are happier overall. They are much happier when they can overcome their secretive, quiet, and private nature. Letting people get close to them can be challenging, but it helps them in the long run.

Because they tend to see things in black and white, Scorpio moons have an extreme side to their emotional nature. They love and hate with great passion. Their emotional nature is not lukewarm: it's intense or empty. If Scorpio moons care about someone, they will show their strong emotions. Expressing intense emotions in healthy ways brings greater satisfaction. Reflection, relaxation, and deep breathing will help them balance their reactions. Repressing feelings can negatively impact their health. Finding outlets to release their powerful energy helps them feel better.

Scorpio moon people have a strong sense of self and understand their own wants and needs, which makes them happy. They like to be alone and can withdraw from social interactions for periods of time. They enjoy solitude and participating in solo activities.

Being surrounded by strong, confident, and reliable friends inspires them to form a support system. Finding friends and partners who they can rely on is crucial for their well-being. Scorpio moons can be very selective about who they let into their lives. Trust takes time, and they need to observe people's actions because they don't always believe their words. Once they trust someone, they are loyal confidants who can keep a secret. They get tired of doing everything themselves, so finding someone who is as strong as they are is a relief.

Scorpio moon people feel content when they achieve financial independence. Money brings security and enables them to pursue their many hobbies. They have expensive taste and want to enjoy the finer things in life. Feeling successful in their career is tied to a lucrative salary and feeling appreciated for the work they do. Hard workers who are devoted and dedicated to achieving goals, Scorpio moons thrive when they can do a job they love and make good money from it.

SCORPIO MOON TRANSFORMATION

Throughout their lives, Scorpio moons adapt and change into different people. They often feel like they are being reborn. Rebirth is the ability to overcome unexpected life situations; they adapt to challenges by releasing parts of themselves and regenerating their emotions. Scorpio moons are meant to grow stronger through difficult emotional experiences, and shedding their skin, adapting to crises, overcoming adversity, and surviving upheaval are the Universe's gift to them. It is a part of Scorpio moon's soul mission to feel these intense emotions as they grow, experience rebirth, and transform; they have the stamina and strength to overcome every obstacle.

Scorpio moon people are also connected to death. Many experience loss and grief at a young age. Losing loved ones forces them to come face-to-face with the fragility of life. From a young age, they wonder what will happen when they die. This question is difficult to answer, which pushes Scorpio moons to find their own answers. They transform by studying astrology, healing, and new age topics. Processing their dark emotions and expressing them in healthy ways helps them transform. A positive outlet can help them overcome uncomfortable feelings such as jealousy, envy, hatred, and anger. Forgiving others and releasing resentments also helps them move forward.

SCORPIO MOON HEALING

Scorpio moons heal when they can forgive and release the past. Giving people a second chance is not easy for them; cutting people off and moving on without them is one of their coping mechanisms. But holding on to grudges and painful emotions can make them bitter and lead to pent-up anger. Negative emotions will plague their lives if they don't learn how to forgive past hurt.

Scorpio moons are intensely emotional and take things personally. Other people's words affect them deeply, so they are super sensitive to criticism. It's difficult for them to forget how others made them feel. They can hold a grudge and have a hard time forgetting how people treat them. When they realize that no one is perfect and people make mistakes, then they can heal.

Scorpio moons need to feel complex emotions in order to truly understand themselves and others. Refusing to feel emotions, repressing them, and avoiding dealing with them can negatively affect their health. Many Scorpio moons struggle with reproductive issues, health issues involving the sexual organs, and issues of elimination. When they are hurt, they struggle with feelings of depression, isolation, jealousy, and revenge. Healing inner wounds and processing loss can be easier if they talk to a trained counselor or therapist. While Scorpio moons are naturals when it comes to giving other people advice, they rarely seek help for their own problems. They need to realize it's healthy to ask for support. Releasing the burden of dealing with their problems on their own will help them heal many areas of their life.

Healing relationships with friends and family helps them overcome karmic lessons. Trusting others and being more vulnerable are helpful tips for healing. One sign that a Scorpio moon is healing is when they resist the urge to push someone away before truly getting to know them. It takes time to get to know others, and giving people a chance to get close to them helps Scorpio moons build lasting friendships.

SCORPIO MOON RESILIENCY

Emotional survivors who are born with an inner strength, Scorpio moons are able to overcome traumatic situations by utilizing their powerful determination. Overcoming heartbreak, unexpected changes, and roadblocks helps them develop greater resilience. They have a passionate desire to dust themselves off and rise up over and over again—crisis does not hold them back.

Scorpio moons experience emotional rebirths that change them on a soul level. They are the most resilient moon sign and are capable of overcoming situations that many other people struggle to process. They can handle a lot of change and crisis. Rising from the ashes, reborn and renewed, can change them into an entirely new person. They are survivors who regenerate themselves by rising out of painful situations.

Scorpio moons possess an abundance of willpower and do everything in their power to learn from their mistakes. They work hard for what they want and don't back down. They are natural executives because they are ambitious when it comes to reaching their goals. These traits also help them transform traumatic experiences into life lessons.

Scorpio moons have an awareness of how loss and grief impact life. They instinctively support people who are grieving and are natural counselors. People are drawn to them for healing. Extremely intuitive, they are able to understand the emotional pain of others. One of their greatest strengths is their ability to listen to people's problems and give advice. They become more resilient when they assist friends and family who reach out for help.

Patient at heart, they are insightful and carefully plan everything they need to do in order to succeed. They possess the ability to plot future courses of action; they slowly strategize their next move while analyzing others' motives. They read people easily and see right through fakeness. This gift helps them prevent abandonment and disappointment. Their intuitive abilities also help them prepare for change.

Scorpio moons fight hard to defend themselves. They are born with a stinger that comes out when they are in danger. They might appear calm, cool, and collected, but inside their passion is boiling. With that being said, Scorpio moon people have the ability to cut off, kill, and bury their emotions. Denial and refusing to feel ensure they can protect themselves from people who might hurt them. Because of this, they struggle to communicate, even when discussing things like their wants and needs. Feeling vulnerable is scary for them, and they prefer to reflect on their emotions privately. Learning how to forgive others makes them more resilient.

SCORPIO MOON VALUES

Scorpio moons value loyalty. Having faithful and trustworthy friends and partners is crucial for their well-being, but they struggle to find trusted friends, allies, and confidants. They have high standards! It takes them a long time to fully trust anyone, so when they find someone that is loyal, they value that relationship and will sacrifice anything for those they love.

Quiet, perceptive, and observant, Scorpio moon people calculate everything before making a decision. They are focused on the serious side of life. Fakeness and superficiality irritate them. They value genuine people who admit their mistakes and tell the truth. Because of this, they keep their inner circle small. Scorpio moons feel grateful if they have one or two close confidants.

Scorpio moons value intimacy, sexual chemistry, passion, and deep, soul-level relationships. When they fall in love, it's all or nothing—Scorpio moons don't experience lukewarm feelings. Developing trust, feeling comfortable, and allowing themselves to be vulnerable with another can be valuable, but intimate relationships have to be with people on their emotional level. They need to be able to discuss deep and meaningful topics like life, death, and psychological growth with their partner. Because Scorpio moons are cautious about sharing their private feelings, they need a passionate partner who can inspire them to be more open.

Scorpio moons want to obtain a position of authority where they have power over people, decisions, or money. Owning their own business gives them the freedom to make their own choices. They value people who can help them attain their desires. Scorpio moons are ambitious, competitive, driven, and imaginative, and they enjoy financial success because of the independence it brings. Calculating ways to get what they need in order to succeed comes naturally for them. They understand that having money makes life a lot easier and more comfortable—it helps them pursue their goals.

SCORPIO MOON SELF-CARE

Avoiding drama and unnecessary conflict will help Scorpio moon people focus on what is important. Expressing unpleasant emotions helps Scorpio moons release heavy energy. Discussing their problems with someone they trust is key. Spending time with close friends or loved ones helps them unwind. Experiencing intimacy and affection can also relieve stress.

Scorpio moons should use their imagination and creative abilities to turn inward and reflect. Activities that involve quiet time, such as meditation, yoga, and exercise, are helpful. Going to the spa and getting a massage helps Scorpio moons unwind and balance their stress levels. Any activity that can help them express their deepest feelings relieves stress, so they should make time to journal, listen to music, be physically active, or spend time outdoors.

Spending time near water is relaxing and helps Scorpio moons detach from the world. They benefit from relaxing at the beach, swimming, and even soaking in a hot tub or bath.

SCORPIO MOON SELF-CARE PROMPTS

Journaling helps Scorpio moons purge pent-up anger and express their feelings in a safe way.

1. Where do you find passion?

2. What makes you happy?

3. What moon sign traits make you resilient?

4. How do you forgive and let things go?

5. What makes you feel comfortable?

6. How do you handle emotional stress?

7. What is something positive you learned from your mother?

8. What self-care tips are you going to implement?

9. List three things that bring you emotional fulfillment.

10. List three things you are grateful for.

SCORPIO MOON AFFIRMATIONS

- "I forgive others and release the past."

- "Past traumatic experiences made me resilient."

- "I trust others and open up emotionally."

- "I listen to my own intuition."

- "I am a powerful healer."

MOON IN SAGITTARIUS

Nickname: Sagittarius the Traveler

Symbol: The archer

Sun Sign Dates: November 22–December 21

Ruler: Jupiter

Rules: The ninth house; the hips, liver, and thighs

Sign Type: Fire, mutable

Polar Opposite Sign: Gemini

Keyword: "I perceive"

Tips for Healing: Prioritize freedom, travel often, build faith, focus on optimism

Key Traits: Adventurous, restless, optimistic, open-minded, noncommittal, generous

Values: Positivity, faith, travel, adventure, independence, honesty, knowledge

Maslow's Hierarchy of Needs: Social and self-actualization needs

Sagittarius is ruled by the fire element. Sagittarius moons are full of energy and enthusiasm, which helps them accomplish many things. As a mutable sign, they are adaptable and open to change; new ideas, places to visit, and challenges excite them.

Sagittarius moons are adventurous and positive. They wither in a confining or negative environment. Because they like to be active, they have a hard time being cooped up inside; sitting still at a desk, for example, drains their energy. At work, they need trust and autonomy. If they feel like they are being micromanaged, they will quit. Securing a job that allows the opportunity to travel satisfies them and motivates them to work harder. If traveling for work is not an option, they will need to take trips to exotic locations at least once a year. Travel is a priority for Sagittarius moons, and they're especially drawn to international locations. They like to eat ethnic foods and explore different churches, shops, and historic sites. Learning about different cultures fascinates them. They love the outdoors and are drawn to larger animals like horses. Many enjoy riding horses and owning them.

Sagittarius moons have an active mind and prefer to look toward the future instead of dwelling on the past. They always see the bright side of situations. Sagittarius moons are generous, fun loving, boisterous, and like to have a good time. They are known to be party people and enjoy social events. Their sense of humor is charming, and others enjoy being in their presence. Positive energy exudes from them, and they always appear upbeat. They don't want to waste their time surrounded by negativity; if they feel that someone is holding them back, they quickly run off to find someone new.

Sagittarius moons don't have time to wallow in self-pity. They bounce back quickly from adversity because of their ability to see the silver lining in negative situations. And, because they are focused on positive solutions, they have amazing energy to make things happen. Optimistic at heart, they need friends, family, and partners who encourage their enthusiasm.

Generous and kind, Sagittarius moons tend to befriend people who need help because they like to use what they've learned to help others overcome similar situations. Sagittarius moons are supportive and make a positive impact on everyone around them. Friendly, happy, and bright, they have an ability to deliver feedback in a constructive way. They easily recognize other people's strengths, and they make excellent friends due to their honesty. Sagittarius moons are known for their direct, brutally honest communication style— they don't sugarcoat things.

Sagittarius moons are intelligent, witty, and able to discuss a variety of topics. They love to learn new things, so taking classes, pursuing higher education, and mastering new skills makes them happy. They have an interest in knowledge but become restless sitting in a classroom and being forced to learn a certain way. Because of this, some Sagittarius moons drop out of school and don't finish a traditional education. Others go on to obtain multiple degrees, and some even find themselves writing, teaching, and educating others. Even if they never went to college or graduate school, Sagittarius moons are forever students. Avid readers, they absorb ideas easily. Some have photographic memories but decide to learn a trade, like construction, or open their own small business. They are go-getters who aren't afraid of working hard for what they want, and amazing opportunities often fall into their lap.

Sagittarius moons are dreamers and philosophers. They are interested in learning about different belief systems, religions, and values. Connecting to a religious faith is important to them because they believe in the power of prayer. Many Sagittarius moons are born with faith in a higher power. Even if they were not raised in a religious household, many gravitate toward religion. Emotionally, they feel drawn to service, and some are interested in clergy positions, becoming priests, nuns, or deacons of a church. Devotion to a higher power encourages them to seek answers to deep philosophical questions. Sagittarius moons want to know the meaning of life. They believe that everyone has a special purpose, and this helps them support others when they suffer traumatic life situations.

Seeking their own answers to life's problems is second nature for Sagittarius moons—they don't like asking other people for advice. They are confident and trust their own intuition.

Because they need to feel free and independent at all times, Sagittarius moons struggle with intimate relationships. They are perfectly content being single and doing things on their own, so they are known to avoid commitment. Some believe relationships are burdensome and confining. If they can find relationship partners that allow them enough emotional freedom, they might settle down, but many choose to never marry. Having children might be scary for them as they fear losing their freedom. They prefer having the flexibility to travel, move, or change jobs whenever they want to. If they do become a parent, they are known to be adventurous and active, and they will encourage their children to learn, explore the world, and travel. As a parent, Sagittarius moons give their children tons of room to roam and encourage autonomy to find their own interests.

Sagittarius moon people need passion, variety, and excitement in their romantic relationships. Above all, they need someone who can carry on a good conversation. Intellectual people grab their attention because they enjoy discussing topics such as history, religion, and law. Many Sagittarius moons date and/or marry someone from a different religion or cultural background. But even when Sagittarius moons truly care about someone, they never fully commit. They strive to maintain a sense of separateness from those closest to them. Rebellious and tenacious souls, they like to shake things up when they feel bored.

If a Sagittarius moon had a mother figure present in their life, she might have had these traits, as the moon represents the mother. Sagittarius moon's mother figure was seen as adventurous, straightforward, independent, and intelligent. She probably traveled or moved around and stayed active. She liked to feel the wind in her hair, attend concerts, and socialize with a variety of people. Always on the go, she did not sit still for long. Traditional religion or new age concepts were things she might have believed in or taught. If she was religious, attending church as a family was important to her. During Sagittarius moon's childhood, their mother encouraged positivity and spending time outdoors. Traveling overseas, taking family vacations, and trying new foods were part of the home life. Maybe her friends were from different countries, or multiple languages were spoken within the home.

HOW THE FULL MOON AFFECTS SAGITTARIUS MOON

Sagittarius moon people have extra energy during a full moon, which makes them feel more restless. Normally, they are on the move and active, but this heightened restlessness makes them unable to focus. If they can harness the full moon's energy, they will be able to accomplish many tasks they have put off.

Emotions will be heightened during this time. Sagittarius moons may experience irritability, frustration, and feeling more on edge than usual. Some might feel withdrawn and have difficulty being around people. If they feel sad or negative during the full moon, Sagittarius moons pull themselves out of it by focusing on the future. Their positivity helps them during this time. Their motto is "This too shall pass," and they can find hope in any situation.

FINDING PASSION

Sagittarius moons find adventure and passion in many situations. Driving around and listening to music with the windows rolled down brings them joy. Attending concerts, spending time outside, partying, and socializing are enjoyable. Being able to share their thoughts with others is important to them. They like a healthy debate that challenges their beliefs.

Sagittarius moon people like to discuss faith, history, politics, and human behavior. Mental challenges energize them and help them expand their mind. They are passionate about knowledge, so reading, studying, and learning new things excites them. Broadening their horizons by traveling or learning a new language interests them. Encouraging others to explore different cultures, beliefs, and philosophies brings passion.

Sagittarius moons are naturally confident. They walk their own unique path and dislike anything that stifles their inner passion. Conforming to other people's wishes spurs their adventurous spirit to break free.

Like most people, Sagittarius moons enjoy flirting, dating, and being in love. However, they often avoid commitment because it scares them. They don't want to feel dependent on others or be forced into doing things. They are passionate about maintaining a sense of independence in all relationships, romantic or otherwise.

FINDING EMOTIONAL FULFILLMENT

Sagittarius moons need total freedom to feel fulfilled. Personal space and the ability to explore the world are crucial for their emotional well-being. Physical and mental independence allows them to explore new hobbies, embrace change, and pursue adventure. Sagittarius moons value variety; they need to be able to change their mind at the last minute because they want to live in the moment. Restless spirits, they always need something to look forward to, so making vacation plans is comforting.

Sagittarius moon people have a rebellious nature and break free from restrictions. Emotional freedom is needed in all their relationships in order for them to make a commitment. They like to do what they want without having to worry about others. Feeling free to explore is crucial, even when they are in a committed partnership; if anyone or anything makes them feel trapped, they will cut ties.

Sagittarius moons love to tell people what they really think and believe. They are able to tell people the harsh truth in a kind way, which is one of many talents they possess. They want people to grow and find fulfillment, so whenever they can, they help others open up their minds. Sagittarius moons are not afraid to disagree with people or debate a topic they are passionate about.

Because Sagittarius moons are open-minded and understanding, they appreciate being able to express their beliefs and opinions freely and without judgment. Sagittarius moon people are restless souls who need to surround themselves with upbeat and positive people. They would rather be alone than spend time with negative or pessimistic partners.

Emotional fulfillment can also be found by reading and learning new things. Sagittarius moons are always seeking knowledge and pushing their mind to new limits.

SAGITTARIUS MOON COMFORT

When Sagittarius moons believe in a higher power, they feel comfort. Faith and hope are always at their fingertips. They can find the good in any situation. Sagittarius moons avoid conflict and negativity whenever possible; being around like-minded people is comforting.

Comfort for Sagittarius moons is tied to their sense of freedom. They feel comfortable when they can explore new places and meet new people. Autonomy and self-reliance bring comfort. Action is also comforting for Sagittarius moons; they are physically active and enjoy running errands, driving from place to place, and exploring new areas. Inner restlessness moves them forward and pushes them out of their comfort zone. Silencing their mind and resting can be challenging because they are always on the go, but slowing down is beneficial from time to time.

SAGITTARIUS MOON HAPPINESS

Sagittarius moons have a restless soul that seeks knowledge and wisdom. Broadening their mind via travel, study, literature, and new connections brings contentment. Gaining knowledge about the meaning of life is deeply fulfilling. Pursuing a spiritual path brings happiness and helps Sagittarius moons find their purpose.

This is one of the happiest moon signs. Sagittarius moon people are born with an ability to adapt to negative experiences without getting stuck in the past. Being grateful and appreciating what they have enables them to keep a positive outlook. They always count their blessings and enjoy reminding others to do the same. They radiate happiness to people around them. Sagittarius moons are unapologetically themselves, and not caring what people think about them is a gift.

Sagittarius moons are friendly and enjoy spending time with other people. Their happiness is connected to their environment, so it's important for them to surround themselves with like-minded people who inspire their exuberant energy. They are excellent at giving advice and motivating others to focus on the positive; helping others solve problems makes them feel needed and brings happiness.

Sagittarius moons don't like depending on other people to take care of their needs; being self-sufficient comes naturally, and they strive to maintain control over their own life. The freedom to choose their own path and make their own decisions is important to them. They thrive when they are able to do what they want to do. They seek adventure and need to feel like they can grow. Sagittarius moons are happiest when they can be adventurous and experience the rush of excitement in learning something new. Travel makes them happy. Financially, they want to be successful enough to explore all the exotic places they want to see. Being able to wander without a plan makes them happy. They can be found backpacking across Europe or riding a train through multiple states to see the scenery.

SAGITTARIUS MOON TRANSFORMATION

Sagittarius moons transform naturally because they are seekers of new experiences. Difficult life situations do not hold them down for long. Sagittarius moon people have an ability to adapt based on an inner faith. Their faith helps them overcome loss, grief, trauma, and unexpected change, and their personality traits help them bounce back from things that might take others much longer to overcome.

They are luckier than most moon signs. Good luck and fortune come their way, and this helps them in many areas of life. Their positive attitude attracts everything they want. Surrounding themselves with happy people helps them stay motivated, and they can transform the lives of others with their infectious energy and smile.

Making commitments and appreciating stable relationships help them overcome their fears of being tied down. Committed relationships should not be seen as a negative thing; shifting that belief and recognizing that making commitments can actually help them is a lesson they need to learn. When Sagittarius moons realize that they can be connected to others without feeling trapped, they will grow stronger.

SAGITTARIUS MOON HEALING

Sagittarius moons heal when they are able to pursue knowledge. Reading and taking classes soothes their soul. Discussing serious topics such as religion, philosophy, and world issues helps them heal. Researching life's complex problems helps them gain understanding.

Spending time outdoors is beneficial. Hiking, rock climbing, and exploring caves can help Sagittarius moons clear their mind. Spending time in the forest, camping, and renting a cabin are good getaways for healing and reflecting.

To feel balanced, they must nurture their need for adventure. Exploring the world can be extremely healing. Driven and with an abundant amount of energy, movement is soothing to Sagittarius moons and helps them process their thoughts and emotions. Being cooped up in an office or at a desk restricts their energy.

Because Sagittarius moons are always on the go, they can distract themselves from their emotions. Keeping busy can prevent deeper healing if they refuse to slow down and contemplate or process their inner feelings. Sagittarius moon people heal by sitting still and grounding themselves. They also benefit from taking other people's advice; sometimes they believe they know more than others or have already made up their mind.

Typically, Sagittarius moons are optimistic and friendly, which helps them quickly move forward from adversity. They heal when they realize they don't always have to put a smile on their face. Being bubbly, happy, and positive comes naturally most of the time, but Sagittarius moon people need to remember that it's okay to have a bad day. To heal, they need to allow themselves to vent, cry, and complain. Then, after they've fully processed the situation, they can snap back to their upbeat self.

Sagittarius moons are direct communicators who are blunt and honest. Their ability to talk about difficult situations is a strength that helps them confront issues head-on. They heal by expressing their thoughts and emotions. Allowing themselves enough time to feel unpleasant emotions, as well as discussing them with people they trust, helps aid the healing process.

They dislike feeling tied down and heal when they shift their beliefs about freedom. Sagittarius moon people can maintain freedom no matter what other people do or what situations impact their lives.

SAGITTARIUS MOON RESILIENCY

Sagittarius is one of the most resilient moon signs. Overcoming adversity comes easily for them because they are always thinking about the future with a positive attitude. They don't get stuck in the past or hold on to their pain like some moon signs. Moving forward comes naturally for them; they forgive easily and never hold a grudge.

Sagittarius moons believe bad things happen to make them stronger. This optimistic attitude helps them overcome loss, grief, and heartbreak. They refuse to succumb to negativity or let life get them down. Challenge is seen as an adventure. Change is exciting and motivates them to keep pushing toward their goals. Their curiosity and love of new things helps them grow stronger as a person. Sagittarius moons snap out of depression quickly because they believe that things will get better; their inner hope makes them more resilient. Practicing gratitude helps them overcome any situation.

Sagittarius moons grow more resilient when they allow themselves to depend on others. They are extremely self-reliant and don't want to feel dependent on anyone, but they need to learn they don't have to do everything on their own. They would benefit from allowing others to help them. Life will improve once they develop long-lasting friendships and committed relationships. Having someone to talk to about their problems takes a huge burden off their shoulders.

SAGITTARIUS MOON VALUES

Sagittarius moons value positivity, optimism, and focusing on the good things in life. Finding solutions to problems motivates them. Energetic and action oriented, they don't let anything stand in their way.

Life is full of adventure, and Sagittarius moons love to explore. They value the freedom to do what they want. Being self-sufficient and having control over their own schedule means a lot to them. They find joy in almost everything. Travel soothes their soul, and most Sagittarius moons have a bucket list of exotic places they want to see before they die. They enjoy exploring new cities, restaurants, and historic sites. Overseas travel interests them because they value opportunities to expand their experience with different languages, cultures, and traditions.

Sagittarius moons are able to uplift others with their forward thinking and direct, straightforward communication. They make excellent friends because they are able to deliver honesty in a kind way. They like to see other people improve and believe that lying limits growth. Brutally honest, they value and appreciate people who tell it like it is. Their time is valuable and they don't like to wait around—they would rather get to the point. They value relationships that allow them to be themselves.

Sagittarius moon people value philosophical ideas and enjoy studying religion. They believe in a higher power and are born with faith that helps them find a greater purpose. Many Sagittarius moons seek a spiritual path and study topics like astrology, tarot, yoga, and energy healing. Sagittarius moon people value knowledge and intelligence and seek out opportunities to pursue higher education. Attending college and taking classes helps them reach their goals. They can also be avid readers who enjoy learning things on their own.

SAGITTARIUS MOON SELF-CARE

Sagittarius moons need to keep busy and embrace newness in their lives. Stagnation weighs them down, and stress and conflict disrupt their natural energy flow. Self-care activities that help them connect spiritually, such as meditation, prayer, and mindfulness, help them live in the present moment.

Being outdoors soothes their soul. They enjoy hiking, mountain climbing, camping, and exploring new places. Activity is crucial for their well-being, but sometimes this creates anxiety or additional problems if they are not taking time to rest and reflect. Always being on the go prevents them from processing and balancing their emotions. Making time to withdraw, relax, and contemplate their daily life helps them take better care of themselves.

Being intentional about how they use their energy and time helps Sagittarius moons feel better. They can utilize their positive energy by creating a gratitude journal. Each morning, before they start their day, they should jot down three things they are thankful for. This activity will keep them connected to their natural optimism.

SAGITTARIUS MOON SELF-CARE PROMPTS

Making time for quiet breaks to write and journal is a positive self-care tool that helps Sagittarius moons connect to their inner emotions.

1. Where do you find passion?

2. What makes you happy?

3. What moon sign traits make you resilient?

4. What helps you commit to another person?

5. What makes you feel comfortable?

6. How do you handle emotional stress?

7. What is something positive you learned from your mother?

8. What self-care tips are you going to implement?

9. List three things that bring you emotional fulfillment.

10. List three things you are grateful for.

SAGITTARIUS MOON AFFIRMATIONS

• "I prioritize travel, exploration, and adventure."

• "My positive attitude makes me resilient."

• "Learning new things makes me happy."

• "My faith helps me overcome all obstacles."

• "I feel free whether I am single or in a committed relationship."

Moon in Capricorn

Nickname: Capricorn the Achiever

Symbol: The goat

Sun Sign Dates: December 22–January 19

Ruler: Saturn

Rules: The tenth house; the knees, joints, and skin

Sign Type: Earth, cardinal

Polar Opposite Sign: Cancer

Keyword: "I use"

Tips for Healing: Find work-life balance, relax, feel your emotions

Key Traits: Responsible, committed, patient, disciplined, pessimistic, materialistic, productive

Values: Legacy, status, structure, money, wealth, authority, achievement

Maslow's Hierarchy of Needs: Social and ego needs

Capricorn moon is ruled by the earth element. Capricorn moons are practical and take things seriously. As a cardinal sign, they are initiators. They like to be in charge and accomplish whatever they set out to do.

Capricorn moons are ambitious, responsible, and one of the hardest-working moon signs in the zodiac. Determined to succeed, they work hard to achieve all their goals. They can accomplish a great deal of tasks in a short amount of time, and their work ethic is something they take pride in. Very few people can keep up with a Capricorn moon once they charge toward a goal. Capricorn moon people are persistent, strong, and calculating when it comes to accomplishing tasks. Productivity is important to them, and they want to see results. They work hard with one goal in mind: reaching the top. Obtaining a successful career is their main priority. Capricorn moons enjoy material success and having nice things, but their true motivation is working hard so they can financially provide for their loved ones.

Natural leaders, Capricorn moons have a good eye for other people's talents. They motivate and encourage others to work hard. Stubborn from time to time, they dislike taking orders from others or being told what to do—they like to be the one deciding what others should do. Capricorn moons enjoy running their own business or working their way up to a high-level leadership position. It might take some time, but because Capricorn moons are patient, they will reach the top. Capricorns are financially clever and have a good business sense.

Capricorn moons want success but sometimes feel no matter how hard they work, they won't achieve it. They believe they went to the school of hard knocks; in their eyes, nothing was easy for them: everything they've accomplished is the result of hard work, determination, and sacrifice. Capricorn moons know what it's like to struggle to survive. Many experienced the world as a harsh place when they were younger. They believe the world is a place where they have to fight in order to get by. Their self-esteem is tied to their success.

Capricorn moons need to be careful about neglecting their own emotional needs by making work their life's focus. There is more to life than their career. This is hard for them to accept because they get emotional satisfaction from achievement, but work-life balance is important in order for Capricorn moons to truly find happiness.

Other people think Capricorn moons are older than they really are, and it's true they are old souls. Because they are super responsible and serious, they often feel like they are from a different time period. Traditional and old-fashioned, they are attracted to high-quality people and professional behavior. They are known to dislike social situations because they feel uncomfortable when they are forced to talk to strangers. Dating can be challenging for them due to their shy nature. Capricorn moons are not the type to date around; they like committed relationships. They value tradition and may have strong beliefs about roles in relationships. For instance, they will want to pay for their own meal or treat others. Some like to open doors and are known to be chivalrous. They are conservative and get along best with people who are loyal, hardworking, and dependable. At first, Capricorn moons have a cautious and distrusting manner, but once they develop a friendship, they are great at providing practical advice. Underneath their somber exterior, they like to have a good laugh. Witty and sarcastic, they are able to catch people off guard with an inappropriate joke or comment. Their dry sense of humor helps them overcome emotionally challenging times.

Capricorn moons have great pride and refuse to ask anyone for help. They want to be responsible and do things on their own, even if it means they will struggle more. They refuse to take money from anyone or ask for financial help. Capricorn moon people would rather work three jobs than ask for a handout. Ironically, they are generous and happily loan money to family and friends who are struggling. Deep down, Capricorn moons root for the underdog. They like people who are rough around the edges. It is easy for Capricorn moons to spot others' strengths and talents and find a way to nurture them. Once Capricorn moons trust someone, there is nothing they would not do for them, but they expect loyalty in return.

Meeting new people and having to socialize can be stressful for Capricorn moons because they are introverted. They would rather surround themselves with a handful of friends whom they know they can trust. Respectful of authority, tradition, and their elders, Capricorn moons prefer spending time with people who are older and wiser than they are. Many have intimate relationships with people who are much older than them.

Capricorn moons experience challenges in intimate relationships. They are insecure about expressing emotions and hold back their feelings, and most are uncomfortable with affection. Rigidity and a natural shyness can get in the way of true intimacy. They cut people off and repress emotions so they don't have to deal with them; partners may accuse them of being cold and unfeeling. Capricorn moon people cringe and pull away if loved ones try to force affection on them. It's important for them to understand that family and friends need affection even if they don't.

Capricorn moons never want to feel vulnerable or exposed. They don't like showing affection or emotions in public. Having control over their feelings and image is very important to them. Capricorn moons believe emotions can be untrustworthy; they prefer practical, realistic solutions to problems. Emotions make them uncomfortable. My brother and daughter are Capricorn moons, and they both have the classic trait of overthinking their emotions. They both worry about social situations, work, and family.

Capricorn moons withhold emotion because they want to appear stoic and in control, but this can lead them to get stuck in pessimistic thinking patterns that impact their outlook on life. Capricorn moons can suffer from depression and are known to have dark emotional cycles. It is common for them to feel irritable and withdrawn. They are known to lash out at their loved ones when they experience these dark moods. The culprit is typically their own negative thinking.

Most people believe they have it all together, but Capricorn moons are experts at hiding what they feel. They want to appear strong and in control of every area of their life; they care about what other people think and don't want to appear weak. If they feel unstable, unprepared, or caught off guard, they won't show it, though it will affect their ability to complete tasks.

Capricorn moons dislike change and need a solid routine to follow. Planning for the future is extremely important to them. Many Capricorn moons have a gift for managing money and helping others solve practical issues with common-sense solutions. Sarcasm and an uncanny sense of humor help them make light of difficult situations.

If a Capricorn moon had a mother figure present in their life, she might have had these traits, as the moon is associated with the mother. Capricorn moon's mother figure was seen as hardworking, responsible, practical, and strong. She was organized and managed several activities at once. Taking care of the household might have come last because she was busy achieving goals and focusing on her career. She might have traveled a lot for work and left many responsibilities for Capricorn moons to fulfill in her absence. The mother figure taught Capricorn moons the value of money, working hard, and being responsible, as well as the importance of loyalty. Realistic and productive, she wanted her family to learn that things don't come easily. A strong work ethic and high standards were common, which can cause Capricorn moons to be hard on themselves later in life.

HOW THE FULL MOON AFFECTS CAPRICORN MOON

Capricorn moons feel more emotional during a full moon. Typically, they feel cut off from their emotions, so this is a difficult experience for them. Feelings of depression, irritability, and sadness are common. Capricorn moon people are not comfortable with strong emotions and will feel more vulnerable during this time. It is crucial for them to find a positive outlet to express pent-up feelings; if they don't find it, they are likely to experience stressful blowups, disagreements, and arguments.

Capricorn moons need stability, so doing something practical helps them find balance. It would be beneficial to exercise and stay physically active during the full moon.

During a full moon, Capricorn moons will want to withdraw and isolate at home even more than usual. Withdrawing is a way they protect themselves and recover. They might not want to talk to anyone because they can't find the words to match their feelings, but talking to someone they trust can help Capricorn moons process things during this time.

FINDING PASSION

Capricorn moons are passionate about attaining success and achieving career goals. Ambitious at heart, they feel alive when they get recognized for the work they accomplish. Securing a position of power and reaching the top of the career ladder are goals that ignite their desires and energize them; it gives them something to look forward to and something to achieve.

Capricorn moons are passionate about controlling things and having structure. They need stability and a plan of action in order to feel productive. Passionate about to-do lists and flowcharts, they have an ability to map out the future in detail. Patient, steadfast, and long-suffering, they wait for things to manifest at the right time. They hate being rushed and are very patient.

Commitment and traditional relationships help Capricorn moons express their sensual feelings and inner passion. Ideally, they desire a stable partner who has a good career. They are not flirtatious, so dating can be uncomfortable for them. Meeting people through work is common. Capricorn moons want a successful partner and have high standards. Being able to provide financially and materially for their loved ones gives Capricorn moons a sense of purpose. Born with a sense of duty, saving money helps them feel in control. They want to own a nice car and beautiful home, but debt frightens them, and they dislike being dependent on banks. Paying for items with cash is common because Capricorn moons dislike the stress of owing anyone money.

They are passionate about making other people feel better and alleviating uncomfortable social situations; they enjoy making people laugh with a quick joke or sarcastic comment.

FINDING EMOTIONAL FULFILLMENT

Feeling appreciated for the work they do satisfies Capricorn moons. Many Capricorn moons feel they have to work harder than everyone else in order to advance. It may take them longer to move up the ladder, but their patience helps them remain productive and determined to reach the top. Emotional fulfillment is tied to career success, recognition, tangible results, and achievement.

Many Capricorn moons struggle to find emotional fulfillment in their early years. As they get older, they develop greater wisdom and start seeing progress. Capricorn moons are super responsible and carry heavy burdens privately. If they struggle, they resist seeking help because of their pride. They can feel lonely and withdrawn. Sometimes they get stuck in their own head. Finding a true friend who they can trust and rely on will fulfill their desire for companionship.

Learning how to relax and let their hair down can be difficult for Capricorn moons. They dislike being rushed, loud noises, and people who talk too much. They don't like to stand out. Practical and realistic, they find fulfillment in the material world.

Capricorn moons are known to dwell on problems and insecurities. They have high standards for themselves and when something goes wrong, they obsess over it. Worrying can affect their mood. Shifting their focus onto things that are going well and shifting negative thinking increase emotional contentment.

Financial security is important to Capricorn moons because they like to take care of their family. If they are a parent, they will want to provide only the best for their children.

CAPRICORN MOON COMFORT

Capricorn moons are most comfortable when they have financial security and a well-paying job. A stable life with structure, order, and routine suits them best. Having a stable routine helps keep them on track. They like making lists, being prepared, and knowing what to expect in every situation. Capricorn moons have a realistic, down-to-earth attitude, which helps them feel grounded.

Capricorn moons don't trust their emotions because they are changeable. They need time to think and reflect. Completing tasks and being productive might be where they shine, but they need to work on connecting with their inner emotions. It is difficult for them to show their sensitive side, but they are very caring people. They need to realize that feeling things does not make them weak. Learning to get more comfortable with their emotions helps them in every area of life.

Being in a committed relationship and sharing their life with a reliable partner brings comfort. They need to surround themselves with calm people who can help them relax and unwind. Partnering with someone who is similar to them would be wise, but Capricorn moons often attract partners with opposite personality traits. They like a challenge, so they sometimes get involved with people who take advantage of them. But drama disturbs them, and instability in their relationships greatly affects their overall sense of balance. This type of coupling is painful for Capricorn moons. They are most comfortable in a committed, stable, traditional relationship with someone they admire.

CAPRICORN MOON HAPPINESS

Success makes Capricorn moons happy. Recognition for the practical things they do, both at work and at home, is important.

They like to feel respected, valued, and appreciated for the effort they put in. They feel happiest when they are in a leadership role. Public opinion greatly impacts their self-esteem.

Having a positive attitude and learning not to be so hard on themselves helps relieve stress. Capricorn moon people have high standards that can be hard to live up to; loving and accepting their own flaws helps them achieve greater happiness.

Capricorn moons like to have a sense of purpose. Feeling useful is important to their emotional well-being. Feeling like they are making a difference is important, so they enjoy helping other people obtain their goals. They make excellent mentors and supportive coworkers.

Even though work is extremely important to them, Capricorn moons are most content spending time at home with their family. Having loyal and reliable friends makes them happy. They appreciate people who are honest and trustworthy. If they don't trust someone, they will never open up. Capricorn moons have a sensitive side underneath their hard exterior that only those closest to them get to see.

Capricorn moons often find greater happiness as they get older. Maturity and life lessons help them appreciate what they had to go through to succeed. They work hard to succeed and, in the end, they will reap the rewards. Some say Capricorn moons age backward because they learn to have more fun in later life.

CAPRICORN MOON TRANSFORMATION

Capricorn moons transform when they feel needed. They have a desire to be recognized and respected by others. While this may be important to them, they need to learn to value themselves first.

Determined, focused, and driven, they work hard to achieve all of their goals. Capricorn moons are emotionally steady and determined to patiently move forward. They need to put extra effort into having a work-life balance; work is not everything, and once they realize this, they transform.

Strong, reliable, and responsible, Capricorn moons transform when they learn to have fun. They take things too seriously and can become rigid—this prevents them from enjoying life! Making money is part of life, and we all need to pay the bills, but Capricorn moons tend to get bogged down with responsibilities. Being responsible comes naturally for them, and they feel like they have to take care of everyone. They need to remember that life is meant to be enjoyed too. Prioritizing tasks and focusing on what is most important can help them implement more downtime into their schedule. Change can be scary for Capricorn moons, but they grow stronger when they embrace it.

When they can focus more on the present moment, they transform. It's easier to enjoy life when they allow themselves to feel what is happening right in front of them. Being present helps them connect emotionally with those they love. Capricorn moons need to embrace the fact that people are more important than productivity. Nurturing relationships with coworkers, family, and friends is more important than completing mundane tasks.

CAPRICORN MOON HEALING

Capricorn moons heal when they value their personal life more than their work life. Spending quality time away from work with family, children, and friends helps them find emotional balance.

Capricorn moons are known to experience depressive mood cycles. It is important for them to focus within when these feelings arise. Healing insecurity and the belief that they are not good enough helps them overcome self-doubt. No one can be perfect all the time; Capricorn moons need to accept themselves and others without judgment. Releasing their critical beliefs and opinions helps them heal.

Capricorn moons need to heal their relationships. Loved ones often feel neglected because of how much time Capricorn moons spend working. And if things aren't going well at work, they sometimes take it out on their family. When they interact with their loved ones, Capricorn moons need to make sure they are not distracted and fully present. They heal when they realize people are more important than completing tasks.

Capricorn moons need to heal the belief that they have to be successful in order to be worthy. From time to time, they need to detach from their responsibilities, release their high standards, and prioritize relaxation. Controlling their emotions and other people will only cause difficulty; instead, they need to release the reins once in a while. Life is full of change, and once they stop resisting it and go with the flow, they feel better. Capricorn moons heal when they can laugh, have fun, and get their mind off of practical matters.

CAPRICORN MOON RESILIENCY

Capricorn moons become more resilient by utilizing their natural patience. They are willing to work slowly and are able to wait for positive results. Step by step, they focus on the future and where they want to go. Time is on Capricorn moon's side, and they are able to grow stronger and wiser based on life experiences.

Not everything comes easily for Capricorn moons, and this makes them resilient. No matter what life throws at them, they work hard and don't give up. Their maturity helps them bounce back after a crisis. They like rooting for people who struggle because they know what it is like to overcome adversity. They respect people who are resilient, determined, and self-reliant.

Because they are old souls, Capricorn moons use their intuition to make good choices and know how to work with other people. Getting what they want comes easily because they are wise and understand human behavior. Emotionally reserved, they are observers who wait patiently in the wings until the time arrives for them to step out and share their wisdom.

CAPRICORN MOON VALUES

Conservative at heart, Capricorn moons value tradition. Financial success is comforting and is one of the most valuable things to them. Making enough money to provide for their family enhances their self-esteem. Some Capricorn moons work more than one job to produce a steady income in order to afford the things they want. Capricorn moons value anything that stands the test of time. Leaving a legacy motivates them to continue to work hard.

Capricorn moons respect self-made people who worked for what they have. They value conversations with people who are older than them, and they respect experience more than education. They would rather hire someone with hands-on experience than someone with a lot of letters behind their name, because they value grit, strength, and perseverance.

Capricorn moons do value status, and just like the mountain goat, they are always trying to reach the top of the mountain. They value holding a position of authority where they can make real changes; supervising others and leading groups are where they shine. Capricorn moons are good with managing people and financial matters. They are born with a natural business sense and dislike taking orders from anyone else—being a supervisor or owning their own business brings contentment.

Capricorn moons usually start out at the bottom of the food chain and have to work harder than others to reach a high-level position. Even when they've reached the top, they will always remember where they came from. Capricorn moons value dedicated workers and people who are not afraid to get their hands dirty. Respect is key for them, and they value integrity.

Capricorn moons need to feel successful. They work best in a structured environment and dislike disorganization and laziness. Extremely grounded and responsible, they are good at organizing even the most chaotic of environments. They take great pride in their work ethic, their ability to get things done, and their organizational skills. Rules, order, structure, and plans are things they find valuable.

CAPRICORN MOON SELF-CARE

Capricorn moons benefit from taking time off work. They often overwork themselves in order to keep a distance from their emotions. Avoiding problems by staying busy is a way they distract themselves; they put their career first and neglect other areas of their life. Focusing more on their personal life is beneficial for self-care; they should spend more time with their partner, children, and friends.

Learning to express their emotions helps relieve stress. Capricorn moons are known to bottle up their feelings and repress them. Serious and quiet, talking about their emotions makes them feel uncomfortable and vulnerable. If they can talk about their problems with someone they trust, or with a trained counselor, they can begin to release heavy burdens.

Having a good laugh is beneficial and helps Capricorn moons express pent-up emotions. They have a witty, sarcastic sense of humor. At times, their sense of humor turns dark and catches people off guard. Joking around helps them break the ice in social situations and relaxes their rigidity.

Being outdoors in nature helps Capricorn moons relax. Spending time in the forest or near mountains is especially beneficial. Grounding exercises and connecting their physical body to the earth can benefit Capricorn moons. Deep breathing and rigorous exercise can also help calm their nerves. They should get massages to help relieve tight, built-up tension. Visiting a chiropractor can help alleviate stiff joints and muscle pain.

CAPRICORN MOON SELF-CARE PROMPTS

Reflecting on thoughts and emotions is an important self-care tip for Capricorn moons. Because they have a difficult time expressing their feelings verbally, journaling is a great option.

1. Where do you find passion?

2. What makes you happy?

3. What moon sign traits make you resilient?

4. How do you handle responsibility?

5. What makes you feel comfortable?

6. How do you handle emotional stress?

7. What is something positive you learned from your mother?

8. What self-care tips are you going to implement?

9. List three things that bring you emotional fulfillment.

10. List three things you are grateful for.

CAPRICORN MOON AFFIRMATIONS

- "I balance my work and home life."

- "I make time to feel my emotions."

- "I release the tendency to take myself too seriously."

- "Rest is productive too."

- "I show others how I truly feel."

MOON IN AQUARIUS

Nickname: Aquarius the Humanitarian

Symbol: The water bearer

Sun Sign Dates: January 20–February 18

Ruler: Uranus

Rules: The eleventh house; the ankles and circulatory system

Sign Type: Air, fixed

Polar Opposite Sign: Leo

Keyword: "I know"

Tips for Healing: Feel things, connect to others, express individuality

Key Traits: Eccentric, free-spirited, humanitarian, inventive, innovative, detached, aloof, intellectual

Values: Innovation, creativity, individuality, uniqueness, freedom, knowledge

Maslow's Hierarchy of Needs: Social and self-actualization needs

Aquarius is ruled by the air element. Aquarius moons are smart, aloof, innovative, and able to master intellectual challenges. As a fixed sign, they like structure and order. They have trouble changing direction once they have chosen a certain path.

Naturally social, friendly, and charming, Aquarius moon people attract many friends. They are very outgoing and like to spend time with others. Being part of a group is important to them. Humanitarians at heart, Aquarius moons enjoy helping others and have an altruistic nature. Ensuring that everyone is treated equally is something they are passionate about. Helping others on a large scale interests them. Many Aquarius moon people become social workers, missionaries, psychologists, counselors, or healthcare workers. Aquarius moons are sympathetic listeners who are able to ground people when they are upset; their ability to interact with people in an impersonal way makes them a great fit for career fields that others might shy away from. They can detach from their emotions, which enables them to listen and help others in a practical way. Aquarius moons can stabilize crisis situations due to their ability to stay calm, cool, and collected.

Aquarius moons can listen to people's problems without getting overwhelmed because they have good emotional boundaries. There is a silent, detached, and observant quality to their emotional nature. Aquarius moons never get too emotional about anything—they prefer thinking over feeling. They are balanced emotionally and mentally, so they rarely struggle with emotional extremes. Aquarius moons do well in the medical field, especially as surgeons, because of their ability to detach from the human experience. They are also drawn to radiology because they can specialize in diagnosis and don't have to interact directly with patients but can still help others.

When they help solve complicated problems, Aquarius moons feel invigorated. They have a scientific mind and are often described as eccentric, unique, innovative, and free-spirited. Technology interests them because they are futuristic thinkers; they're interested in the unknown and what lies ahead. Highly intelligent, Aquarius moon people come up with out-of-the-box ideas that are ahead of their time.

Aquarius moons are focused on ideas, but they don't like putting in the hard work required to make their dream a reality. Aquarius moon people are unpredictable; they are known to change their mind quickly and don't like to commit to a certain course of action. They can be restless and crave freedom. Original thinkers, they do well in fields such as research, engineering, science, and mathematics.

Another side of Aquarius moons is drawn to philosophy, religion, art, and literature. Avid readers, they like to obtain knowledge about many different subjects. They are forever students who are always picking up new skills and broadening their minds. Aquarius moon people are fast learners, and many have a photographic memory. But they need room to explore, so they become rebellious in traditional classroom settings. Monotony bores them; they need some excitement.

Aquarius moons believe in individuality and original thinking. Standing out in a crowd, being eccentric, and expressing their unique ideas intrigues them. Aquarius moons won't conform to other people's rules; they have a strong-willed side to their airy personality. They feel invigorated when they buck authority, question the rules, and rebel. Challenging other people's dogmatic beliefs is something they are not afraid to do, even if it makes other people uncomfortable.

Aquarius moons either choose not to have children or desire having several children. They make supportive parents and encourage their children to express their creativity and originality. Freedom is important to them, and they give the same respect to their children, partner, and friends.

Intuitive and imaginative, some Aquarius moons are drawn to religion and have a conservative side to their nature. Whether or not they are religious, they enjoy discussing conspiracy theories and studying taboo topics. Some Aquarius moons even experience unexpected flashes of insight about future events, making them clairvoyant, but they tend to doubt these unexplainable experiences.

One interesting thing about Aquarius moons is that even when they have a very traditional belief system, they are independent spirits who want to explore. They like to push the limits of traditional society, especially their parent's rules. Some might get a tattoo or body piercing just to shock friends and family. Likewise, Aquarius moons will rebel if they feel family, friends, coworkers, or lovers are forcing them to do something. If they commit to something, they want to choose it themselves—they like to decide the parameters.

For Aquarius moons, relationships need to be highly intellectual and unemotional, focused on learning and sharing adventures. A mental connection is needed for there to be the possibility of a romantic relationship. They are attracted to people who are eccentric, rebellious, unique, and creative—normal people don't typically hold their interest for very long. Aquarius moons sometimes pursue people who aren't interested in them because they see it as a challenge.

Aquarius moons are always trying to balance their need for independence and commitment. Exploring new relationships is important to them, but commitment can be challenging because the demands of others often make them feel trapped. They don't like having to live up to other people's expectations. As such, intimate relationships don't tend to last long for Aquarius moons. They dislike neediness, possessiveness, jealousy, and feeling tied down. Many choose to be single and never marry, though they do like to keep lovers as friends if the relationship does not work out. Pursuing friendships is more important to them than pursuing romantic relationships because there is less pressure.

If an Aquarius moon had a mother figure present in their life, she might have had these traits, as the moon is associated with the mother. Aquarius moons may have perceived their mother figure as friendly but sometimes detached, aloof, and intellectual. From an early age, the mother figure had many friends, and she may have participated in important groups. The mother figure encouraged Aquarius moon to express their unique ideas and beliefs. Independence and creativity were nurtured in the home. Intellectual debates and discussions were a family activity. Aquarius moons learned how to express their individuality from their mother; she taught them the importance of accepting their strange, unique, and eccentric style. Aquarius moons often have a special friendship with their mother, as she taught them a lot about the world. If the mother figure was unemotional or not affectionate, Aquarius moons can struggle to express emotions and intimacy.

HOW THE FULL MOON AFFECTS AQUARIUS MOON

Aquarius moons feel restless during a full moon. Doing something physical and being active can help express their restless energy.

They are not normally emotional people, but during the full moon, Aquarius moons might feel things they are not used to feeling. This can become uncomfortable for them, and they will struggle to detach from these unpleasant emotions. Overthinking and overanalyzing their feelings are common during this time. Normally social, they might feel withdrawn and depressive. Aquarius moons will feel better if they talk with trusted friends. They would also benefit from journaling and writing out their thoughts on paper.

FINDING PASSION

Aquarius moons are passionate about learning and opening their minds to new information. Being able to question traditional teachings encourages them to find their own answers. They are on a passionate search for knowledge and truth.

Aquarius moon people feel passionate about being unique, creative, and individualistic. They enjoy making their own decisions and plans. Aquarius moons like to experience variety and have the ability to move freely; they don't like to be a follower or listen to other people's rules. The freer they feel, the more passionate they become about exploring new ideas.

Humanitarians at heart, they are passionate about speaking up for others and being an advocate. They fight for what they believe in and may join a group that advocates for human rights, animal rights, or political reform. Aquarius moons are interested in making a difference in other people's lives; it gives them a sense of purpose. Sharing information, socializing, and developing friendships with those who have a shared goal is important. Brainstorming solutions for world problems is something they are passionate about. They're also passionate about building a large social circle. Networking and connecting with people who can help them reach their goals are things they excel at.

FINDING EMOTIONAL FULFILLMENT

Aquarius moons find emotional fulfillment when they are able to showcase their originality. They don't want to be like everyone else—they enjoy standing out and being different. Being able to voice their opinions and unconventional ideas helps them feel supported. Dressing differently than their peers, expressing their creative side, and showcasing their eccentric nature is fulfilling; Aquarius moons like to see the shocked look on people's faces.

They are unpredictable and changeable, so following their instincts brings fulfillment. Traditional societal expectations can become stifling for Aquarius moons; they need to be able to make their own decisions and live their life on their own terms. Not caring what people think is a blessing because Aquarius moons will continue pursuing their dreams even if they aren't popular.

Sometimes Aquarius moon people prefer to live an untraditional lifestyle, and they feel fulfilled when their family and friends support their choices. They find it hard to settle down, so having an open relationship resonates with them. If they can balance their need for autonomy within intimate relationships, they feel supported. Relationships don't have to be stifling, but they only become fulfilling if Aquarius moons take the time to work on them.

AQUARIUS MOON COMFORT

Aquarius moons feel comfortable when they can keep an emotional distance from others. They dislike drama and strong emotional reactions; they prefer a levelheaded approach to solving personal problems. Easygoing and laid-back, they like to go with the flow in relationships. If a relationship requires too much emotional work, they will end it quickly. They are comfortable being single because they don't like feeling responsible for other people's emotions or problems.

Learning what they want to, coming and going as they please, and not being questioned are important to them. Movement and exploration bring comfort. Unsettling and unexpected life changes don't rattle them as much as other moon signs. They adapt to change naturally—some even feel energized after being blindsided. Aquarius moons feel lighter when they can shed the past and start fresh.

Spending time with friends and acquaintances discussing innovative, eccentric ideas brings contentment. No idea is wrong in their opinion; they will explore all options in order to come up with the best solution. Aquarius moons are most comfortable being part of a group and having friends from all walks of life.

Practical and stubborn once they make their mind up, they want to act. Aquarius moons are restless and changeable: one day they might love you, and the next they want to be alone.

AQUARIUS MOON HAPPINESS

Aquarius moons are happiest when they are making the world a better place. Being part of a group and interacting with their peers makes them feel included. Working toward a common goal that can change people's lives inspires them.

Innovative and philosophical, Aquarius moons are futuristic thinkers. They want to be respected for their intellect and sought after for advice. Knowing more than others makes them feel special.

Aquarius moons like solitude and having time to read and catch up on social trends. They enjoy their own company and doing things alone. Living alone and having time to do what they want makes them happy. Being able to express their artistic talents, playing instruments, or listening to music also brings happiness.

AQUARIUS MOON TRANSFORMATION

Aquarius moons are known to detach from their emotions. Sometimes Aquarius moons seem unapproachable or distant; strong displays of emotion make them uncomfortable. Practicing empathy helps them understand others. Feeling their own emotions can be challenging for Aquarius moons, but when they take time to connect to their inner self, they develop greater self-awareness and transform their cold, aloof persona. Connecting emotionally with others takes practice, but they will find it beneficial. Their natural boundaries help them support others and avoid burnout.

Aquarius moons are sociable and attract many acquaintances, but few people ever get to know them well. They have a superficial charm and friendliness. Gaining support from people who can emotionally, intellectually, or financially help them reach their goals is top priority. Believing they can achieve their dreams is the first step toward getting what they want; when they understand their goals, they can work on manifesting them. Visualizing what they want in the future and reciting affirmations help them transform.

Aquarius moon people need to express their individuality. Their open-mindedness leads them to make friends with people from many different walks of life. They enjoy having relationships with people who are very different from them. If they begin to feel smothered, they push people away, but when they can transform their fear of commitment and develop lasting relationships, they will feel more supported. Aquarius moons don't have to do everything on their own—depending on other people can benefit their life!

Because they are highly intelligent, Aquarius moons like to question things and challenge others' ideas, and they usually believe they are right. Sometimes they push others away with their tendency to argue and mentally spar. Debating ideas and beliefs is something they are passionate about, but when they do it just to prove a point, it can make people feel uncomfortable. When they transform their need to know more than others or to prove their intellectual worth, their relationships will improve.

Transformation happens when Aquarius moons allow others to have their own opinions. They need to learn that forcing their beliefs on others causes division. They don't like when people pressure them to conform, so why would they do it to someone else? Aquarius moons transform when they allow others to disagree with them. Opening themselves up to new ideas helps them become a stronger person.

Since they usually feel different from other people, Aquarius moons transform when they accept themselves fully. One thing Aquarius moon people struggle to embrace is their need for mental stimulation. They need to possess an interest in a topic in order to study it or else they will quickly lose interest. But this need for stimulation can be a strength; for example, Aquarius moons like change because it helps them overcome boredom.

AQUARIUS MOON HEALING

Aquarius moons can be detached from their physical body. It's hard for them to verbalize feelings or process them. They feel more comfortable using logic and intellect to solve problems. When they allow themselves to feel unpleasant emotions, they can heal many areas of their life. They need to stop avoiding emotions and pushing people away. Their need for autonomy and independence can prevent healing.

When Aquarius moons experience loss, they want to think it through to make sense of it. Grief has to be felt, and they need to allow themselves to express emotions. As a mental sign, they overanalyze things, making them feel worse. Sometimes thinking does not help them solve emotional problems. Aquarius moons find practical ways to deal with crisis and change. Being part of a support group with others who have had similar life experiences would be beneficial. They need to avoid isolating themselves when they are struggling with emotional issues. Ultimately, change can inspire them and invigorate them.

Aquarius moons can be independent spirits and still interact with others in emotional ways. Flashes of insight and imaginative ideas hit them out of the blue. Journaling and writing down their ideas, thoughts, and feelings helps them get in touch with what they really want. It also helps them process pain, grief, and unpleasant feelings.

Understanding other people's perspectives and taking time to listen helps them support others. Making friends and communicating important ideas helps them connect and build rapport with other people. Volunteering and helping people who are suffering helps get their mind off their own problems. Focusing on a larger mission and goal helps them move forward in life. Aquarius moons want to make a difference in people's lives, though they don't always know how to show it. They have a good heart, even if they appear cold. Healing comes through communicating and teaching other people what they know.

Talking with friends or loved ones can help them get in touch with deeper emotions. Healing happens when Aquarius moons let people help them solve their problems. Learning to get comfortable with being in committed relationships helps bring emotional stability to many areas of their life. Being patient, dedicated, and reliable helps others trust them. They need to slow down, take a deep breath, and practice being fully present with others.

Overcoming obstacles and developing coping skills helps them focus on the future. Having a creative vision of where they want their life to be helps them heal. They realize they won't be stuck for long and can use their ideas to plan a way to overcome challenges.

Aquarius moons heal by not caring about what expectations other people have for them. Their parents and friends might expect them to feel a certain way and judge them if they don't, but Aquarius moons are happiest when they follow their own chosen path. Pursuing their dreams regardless of what society, tradition, and other people want helps them heal insecurities.

AQUARIUS MOON RESILIENCY

Aquarius moons are resilient and overcome challenges quickly. They bounce back after difficult times and focus on moving forward. Aquarius moon people don't get bogged down in emotions; their practical thinking helps them overcome heartache. Adapting to the unexpected helps them embrace surprises and go with the flow. They keep a positive attitude and look toward the future.

Spending time with trusted friends and pursuing a common goal distracts Aquarius moons from unpleasant feelings. Thinking about others and focusing on their needs helps Aquarius moon people overcome challenges. They are free spirits who use their knowledge and experience to grow stronger. Aquarius moons become more resilient when they refuse to let the opinions of others influence them.

Some Aquarius moon people are religious, devout, and/or follow a spiritual path. Their scientific mind can get in the way of connecting to something outside themselves. They either have faith in a higher power and believe that everything happens for a reason, or they struggle to believe in God. Either way, Aquarius moons become more resilient when they have a spiritual belief system that brings them comfort.

AQUARIUS MOON VALUES

Aquarius moons value innovation. Thinking outside the box and searching for new ways to solve problems is important to them. Talking others through complex problems gives them a sense of purpose. They value mental challenges and brainstorming. Finding unique solutions inspires them. Sometimes other people don't understand their ideas, but Aquarius moons are good at convincing others to open their minds.

Aquarius moon people value being seen as different and one of a kind. A unique sense of style and self-expression helps them express their eccentric tendencies. They walk to the beat of a different drummer and forge their own path. Aquarius moon people value freedom and independence. Some have unconventional relationships or challenge society's standards of what is appropriate. Sometimes people don't understand Aquarius moons, but they value standing out nonetheless.

Aquarius moons value their space in personal relationships. Not being forced to conform to rules or social norms is invaluable to them. If they are able to question and explore unique ways of living and doing things, they find inner satisfaction.

Learning new things and gaining knowledge are the areas Aquarius moon people focus on the most. Reading, researching, and educating themselves stimulates their mind, and Aquarius moons need constant mental stimulation. They value spending time with people who are intelligent. They have strong opinions and enjoy teaching others what they know.

They like to explore a variety of topics, including some that are scientific and others that are new age or nontraditional. Aquarius moons enjoy learning about astronomy, astrology, and alternative medicine. They respect a variety of religions, beliefs, and lifestyles. Aquarius moon people value diversity and anything that is different from how they were raised. Nontraditional beliefs and relationships are important to them.

AQUARIUS MOON SELF-CARE

Focusing on the future energizes and inspires Aquarius moons, but they need to work on being fully present. They detach from their emotions easily, and this can leave them feeling lonely. This personality trait can be a strength that helps them adapt to stress, but it is also a weakness because other people might find them cold or uncaring. Withdrawing and spending time alone helps them center themselves.

Aquarius moons need to do something creative and fun to relieve stress. Solving problems, playing games, putting together puzzles, and participating in intellectual challenges helps them unwind. They also benefit from getting outdoors and exploring. Aquarius moons should spend time in the forest or near mountains, soaking in the fresh air. Spending time in nature helps them relax and balance their thoughts.

Aquarius moon people like mental stimulation, but it's also important to clear their mind from time to time. Meditation and mindfulness exercises can benefit Aquarius moons. Deep breathing exercises, yoga, and stretching helps them soothe their nerves. Studying, reading, and utilizing their creativity helps them find calmness.

Getting out and being social also helps Aquarius moons feel better. Being around groups of people and attending social events is when they feel most supported. Aquarius moons often have unique hobbies, and being part of a special group of like-minded people brings them joy.

AQUARIUS MOON SELF-CARE PROMPTS

Aquarius moons benefit from reflecting on their thoughts and allowing themselves to truly process and experience their emotions.

1. Where do you find passion?

2. What makes you happy?

3. What moon sign traits make you resilient?

4. How do you connect emotionally with others?

5. What makes you feel comfortable?

6. How do you handle emotional stress?

7. What is something positive you learned from your mother?

8. What self-care tips are you going to implement?

9. List three things that bring you emotional fulfillment.

10. List three things you are grateful for.

AQUARIUS MOON AFFIRMATIONS

- "I acknowledge and feel my emotions."

- "I prioritize my freedom and independence."

- "I am unique, and it is one of my greatest strengths."

- "I use my creativity to solve problems."

- "I pay attention to the needs of others without neglecting my own."

MOON IN PISCES

Nickname: Pisces the Mystic

Symbol: The fish

Sun Sign Dates: February 19–March 20

Ruler: Neptune

Rules: The twelfth house; the feet and pituitary gland

Sign Type: Water, mutable

Polar Opposite Sign: Virgo

Keyword: "I believe"

Tips for Healing: Balance emotions, make time to relax, implement boundaries

Key Traits: Idealistic, artistic, compassionate, escapist, receptive, self-sacrificing, imaginative

Values: Kindness, imagination, creativity, sleep, alone time, service, spirituality

Maslow's Hierarchy of Needs: Security and self-actualization needs

Pisces moons are ruled by the water element. They want to help people and are sympathetic to other people's problems. As a mutable moon sign, they adapt to change easily and are easygoing.

Pisces moon people have heightened sensitivity to their environment. They pick up the thoughts and feelings of others. One of the most empathic moon signs, they instinctively take on the pain of others; other people's moods greatly impact them. Because of this, Pisces moons need to prioritize spending time around happy and positive people.

Because Pisces moons like taking care of those who feel lost, they are drawn to the helping professions. They succeed as psychologists, social workers, and spiritual advisors. At work, they tend to zone out, and they need a peaceful, harmonious work environment. Stress, conflict, and disagreements disturb them and affect their ability to get tasks accomplished. They would rather be talking with people, listening and offering advice, or being creative. Mundane, boring tasks will make them feel unhappy. Being a caretaker and comforting others is their forte, but taking care of their own needs is just as important. They must learn to be as kind to themselves as they are to others.

Emotionally, Pisces moons are wide open, and music, art, and human suffering affect them deeply. When they feel people's pain, they want to alleviate it. Pisces moons naturally see the good in people and are idealistic—some might say they see the world through rose-colored glasses—but Pisces moons get hurt by their own illusions. Sometimes Pisces moons feel like others take advantage of their kindness, but they have difficulty standing up for themselves because they avoid conflict. People going through hardship are drawn to Pisces like moths to a flame. To protect themselves, Pisces moons need to develop strong boundaries.

Psychic abilities enable Pisces moons to help people on a deeper level. Meditation comes easily for them, as does tapping into the unconscious. Born with many gifts, dreaming of the future is common for them. Pisces moons would benefit from learning about hypnosis, the Akashic records, astrology, and energy healing. Tarot cards or art therapy are tools that can help them connect to their intuition. They have to develop confidence and learn to trust their special gifts. Trusting their intuition will help them avoid unhealthy people and situations.

Fiercely compassionate, Pisces moons are natural empaths who feel people's pain. This ability makes them excellent counselors, social workers, physicians, and nurses. They also like working with children and animals. They are compassionate and kind souls who sacrifice themselves for others. Pisces moon people are often found working with those who are less fortunate, sick, abused, or neglected.

Pisces moons are dreamy, spiritual souls who want to connect with a higher power. They don't always see things in a practical way. Pisces moon people are interested in finding the meaning of life. They believe in souls and that everyone has a special purpose. Ultimately, Pisces moons are here to discover their destiny and find their soul mate. Faith, hope, and love give them the inner strength they need to overcome crises.

Struggles with sadness, loneliness, and depression are common. Living in the real world can be painful for Pisces moons. They expect others to be kind and get their feelings hurt easily. Unrealistic at times, they might idolize the wrong people. Numbing their emotions can become an unhealthy coping mechanism. Anything that helps them detach from their emotions can become addictive; they need to be careful about using substances such as nicotine and alcohol. Solitude helps them reconnect and find peace.

Pisces moon people have a sensitive nature that makes them want to escape from the world. They like to escape from their problems and have a vivid imagination. When they are able to spend quality time alone, they recharge. Solitary activities help them heal, especially those that are part of a spiritual practice. Pisces moons benefit from meditation, yoga, deep breathing, energy healing, and alternative medicine. If they don't get enough alone time, they can become moody, irritable, and withdrawn.

From a young age, Pisces moons learned the pain of heartbreak and betrayal. Lessons with love and relationships are challenging, but Pisces moons seek a soul mate relationship. Romantic, sensual, and caring, they like to be in love. Being intimate with someone and sharing their inner emotions is comforting. They fall in love easily and find it hard to move on; letting people go can be difficult for Pisces moons. Learning to be more practical helps prevent heartbreak. Pisces moons are idealistic and can ignore red flags in relationships. They forgive easily and give people multiple chances.

Many Pisces moons like having a pet or being around animals or children in some way. If they have children of their own, they will be loving and affectionate and teach their children the importance of expressing their emotions. Pisces moons will encourage their children to explore their imaginative, creative side through art and music.

If a Pisces moon had a mother figure present in their life, she might have had these traits, as the moon is associated with the mother. Pisces moons perceived their mother figure as creative, spiritual, compassionate, and kind. They learned a lot about helping others from their mother. Pisces moons are usually close to their mother and learned from her how to show love. The mother figure encouraged them to express their artistic and musical gifts. At an early age, the mother figure taught them the importance of believing in a higher power. When Pisces moons were younger, they might have attended church with their mother and family. Some learned about astrology, crystals, and new age topics from their mother. If the mother figure was emotionally unstable or emotionally unavailable, Pisces moons might struggle with low self-esteem or lack healthy boundaries.

HOW THE FULL MOON AFFECTS PISCES MOON

Pisces moons experience heightened psychic abilities during the full moon. Their dreams might be more vivid, and they feel more in touch with their intuition. They often feel more devoted to their spiritual path during this time as well.

Escapist tendencies can be heightened, making them want to be by themselves at home. Feeling safe, secure, and comfortable will be important during this time. They might feel anxious, unsettled, and sad, which makes them cry more easily. It is okay to allow themselves to express feelings even if they aren't sure why they are upset.

Pisces moons might feel more sensitive to the environment and other people's energy during this time. Their feelings can become overwhelming, so it's important for Pisces moons to find time to ground themselves. Meditation, breathing exercises, and spending time alone near water can help them balance strong energies. Journaling during this time is another helpful tool. Taking care of their own emotional needs first and trusting their instincts helps them make better decisions in the future.

Pisces moons might feel more creative during the full moon and want to draw, paint, listen to music, or create something new. Tapping into intense emotions can help them finish a creative project they might have put off.

FINDING PASSION

Pisces moons are passionate about making a difference in the world. They are naturally supportive and want to help others. Addicted to feeling needed, they will do anything for someone who asks for their help. The more someone needs their help, the more devoted Pisces moons become. They often feel sorry for other people and recognize when someone is hurting. Sometimes they fall in love with people's pain without realizing it. Neglecting themselves in the process can become dangerous, so they need to practice self-love first. Pisces moons expect other people to be as kind and thoughtful as they are; when they experience the harsh reality that most people are not like them, they feel disappointed, sad, and lonely. Disillusionment with love, romance, and intimacy happens at an early age.

Pisces moons experience periods of sadness and depression. Their emotions are constantly changing, and they wear their heart on their sleeve. Solitude is critical for their emotional balance. Withdrawing from the practical world and having quiet time helps them reflect on their thoughts and emotions. Contemplation allows them to recharge their energy.

Pisces moons are passionate about making friends who share the same interests as they do. Spiritual pursuits such as meditation, mindfulness, breathing exercises, yoga, and learning about metaphysical subjects inspire their imagination. Reading about new age beliefs and exploring divination helps them dig deeper. They want to feel connected to others on a spiritual level. Pisces moons are psychic, and many are passionate about working in this career field.

In order to be intimate with someone, Pisces moons must have a spiritual connection to their partner and share a common belief system. They are attracted to artists, musicians, actors, and creative people. Physical attraction is not as important to them as a soul connection.

FINDING EMOTIONAL FULFILLMENT

Pisces moons find emotional fulfillment by serving others. Helping those that are less fortunate gives them a sense of purpose. They understand other people's emotional pain and are able to empathize. Because they are naturally sympathetic, they enjoy listening to others' problems and giving advice. They understand what people need and are able to comfort others easily.

Expressing their creative and artistic talents helps Pisces moons process their emotions. Listening to music, playing an instrument, or creating a beautiful piece of art are all things they enjoy. If they can make money and provide for themselves financially through these activities, they will be living their dream! Nothing in the material, practical world will fulfill them; they need a deeper sense of purpose and mission in life.

Pisces moon people need to withdraw from the world to deal with stress. Spending time at home doing solitary activities like writing, reading, listening to music, or cuddling with pets helps them feel better. They get overwhelmed by change, chaos, and instability. Quiet time is critical for their emotional fulfillment.

Prayer and meditation help Pisces moons connect to a higher power. They are compassionate souls who need spiritual discipline to help balance their strong emotions. Their faith helps them overcome difficult times.

PISCES MOON COMFORT

Pisces moons are most comfortable in their own home. People create stress for them, which is why they like to spend time by themselves. Solitude allows them to process things and decompress. A quiet, private space in their home where they can relax is necessary for their well-being. Having their own spiritual room or study area where they can make art, read, or write helps them ground their energy and connect within. Surrounding themselves with beautiful art, decorations, and spiritual items such as crystals, angel statues, plants, and soft blankets makes them feel comfortable and safe. Pisces moons benefit from placing a piece of amethyst near their bed or elsewhere in their home. Amethyst is the birthstone for Pisces and provides calming, soothing qualities in the environment. It also helps create better sleep and helps Pisces moons remember their dreams.

Because they are extremely sensitive to energy, they absorb other people's thoughts and emotions. To stay grounded, Pisces moons must avoid drama, stress, and conflict at all costs. Avoiding unhealthy people, negative relationships, and toxic environments is critical for their emotional well-being.

Not having any responsibilities, such as working, cooking, cleaning, or paying bills, comforts them. They like to be able to do nothing so they have time to ponder the meaning of life. Nomads who are seeking a greater purpose, they prefer laid-back environments and people. Pisces moons don't like to feel rushed. They are calm yet adaptable. Because conflict and tension stress them out, they morph into who others need them to be at any given moment. Being a chameleon and getting along with many different types of people brings them comfort.

PISCES MOON HAPPINESS

Not having worldly responsibilities makes Pisces moons happy. The stress of a normal nine-to-five job can burn them out. Taking care of practical things bores them—they would rather be expressing their creative side. Music makes them happy, and many Pisces moons have musical talent. If they don't play an instrument, they certainly will enjoy listening to music.

Attending concerts and dabbling in artistic and spiritual hobbies makes them happy. Being near water is beneficial for Pisces moons; sitting near the ocean, scuba diving, swimming, walking around a lake, and soaking in a hot tub all help soothe their emotions.

Pisces moons are happiest when they are in love. They like romance, excitement, and the rush of being in love. They especially like the feeling of falling in love, when everything is fresh and brand new. They feel love makes life worth living, and they need to have romance in their lives. But once monotony sets in, they can grow restless. Pisces moon people like getting to know someone, and deep down they enjoy the challenge of getting someone to fall in love with them, but they struggle with commitment issues. They swim off when someone new catches their eye. Emotionally changeable, they fall in and out of love frequently. Lovers become friends, as they don't want any relationship to end badly.

PISCES MOON TRANSFORMATION

As empaths, Pisces moon people feel the suffering of the entire world. They are born ultrasensitive to the energy around them, and they unconsciously take on other people's feelings. Being in large groups is uncomfortable because Pisces moons become emotionally overwhelmed. It's best for them to limit large group activity and spend time with a handful of people instead.

Pisces moons attract people who are wounded and need healing. They feel sorry for others and have a bleeding heart. Their energy is compassionate, so others feel drawn to them. Sometimes this makes them a target for selfish people who want to use them. Helping people gives them a sense of purpose and a mission in life, but they can't truly help others if they are not taking care of their own needs first. Sacrifice comes easily for them, but they should never neglect themselves for other people's benefit. Pisces moons transform when they focus on their own needs first. When Pisces moons develop strong boundaries, they can begin to protect their caring heart.

Spending time in solitude is transformational for Pisces moons. They recharge by spending time alone. What others might see as escapist tendencies actually help Pisces moons find peace and security. But avoiding responsibilities and conflict can prevent spiritual growth. Overcoming their selfless emotional nature prevents heartache and benefits them tremendously in the long run.

Following a spiritual path and believing in destiny helps Pisces moons transform. A connection with a higher power helps them work through loss, grief, and disappointment. Meditation and prayer encourage them to calm their mind and overcome worries. Listening to music, reading, writing, and creating are all activities that help them feel better.

PISCES MOON HEALING

Pisces moons heal by listening to music. Music soothes the soul and helps them relax. Being surrounded by art and expressing creativity are also healing.

In order to work on themselves, Pisces moons need to ensure they have a peaceful and stable home life. Having a safe place where they can withdraw, think, write, and ground themselves is key. Spending time alone each day helps them recuperate, process their emotions, and recharge. When they feel overwhelmed or stressed, finding solitude and thinking positively can help them work through negative emotions. Taking care of animals can also encourage healing.

One of the most important things for Pisces moons is feeling a sense of purpose. They need to follow a spiritual path and feel connected to a higher power. Researching different faiths and beliefs can help them find greater meaning in life. They find comfort in the belief that everything happens for a reason, and believing that angels, spirit guides, and a higher power are watching over them is soothing. Spiritual disciplines like yoga, prayer, meditation, breathing exercises, walking, and listening to music inspire healing.

Pisces moons are always sharing their kindness and compassion with others; they are always giving advice and encouraging other people to be strong. Keeping their energy tank full allows them to continue serving others, so it is important they take time to focus on their own life. Pisces moons need to learn grounding techniques. Being present and fully settled in their physical body helps them adjust to outside influences. They are especially vulnerable because they absorb everything around them. Without strong boundaries, they are susceptible to others' thoughts and feelings. As they get overly run down, their immune system weakens, and they can become sick. When Pisces moons stop neglecting themselves, they can truly begin the healing process. Maintaining a healthy routine, eating a balanced diet, making time for exercise, and practicing gratitude all help Pisces moon people maintain their emotional health.

PISCES MOON RESILIENCY

Pisces moons find strength in others. When they feel supported, they can overcome any challenge. Having a supportive group of spiritual friends who have similar goals and passions is crucial, though this can be hard to find. Pisces moon people often feel lonely, though feelings of sadness and loneliness typically motivate them to help others. Deep down, Pisces moons want nothing more than to feel a deep connection with someone. Being in love inspires them to be resilient and push through difficult times. Once Pisces moons learn that they are strong on their own, and that they can and should stand up for themselves, they will have better control over their emotional ups and downs.

Overcoming the belief that they are a victim will help Pisces moons grow stronger. Pisces moons need to believe that everything happens for a reason, which helps them move on. Connecting with a higher power can help them work through unpleasant experiences and overcome adversity. Crisis situations test their strength and show them that they are able to survive any tragedy. Overwhelming emotions and practical matters often make them feel like running away, but believing in destiny and trusting that a higher power has a plan for them helps Pisces moons pick themselves up, dust off, and start over again. They have to let go of the past and learn from their mistakes in order to move forward. Some Pisces moons believe that they experience adversity and crises as a reminder to focus on their spiritual path.

Helping other people makes Pisces moons feel like they have a clear mission in life, but focusing on other people's problems is a coping mechanism they sometimes use to distract themselves from their own problems. Pisces moon people need to ensure they have a healthy balance of giving and receiving in their lives.

PISCES MOON VALUES

Pisces moons value compassion. Being of service and sacrificing their own needs for others makes them feel good. Pisces moons love sharing acts of kindness with their loved ones and taking care of them when they are sick or stressed. Showing other people that they care comes naturally, and they value having family and friends who reciprocate affection and kindness. Sometimes Pisces moons feel they are always providing emotional support to others and not receiving any support in return. They function best when they surround themselves with practical, realistic, and stable friends.

Pisces moons are artistic and sensitive souls that enjoy detaching from the stressors of the world. They have a vivid imagination that helps them create beautiful music and art. Beauty and creative people inspire them to express their own talents.

Stability and routine help balance Pisces moons. Spending time by themselves every day is one the most valuable things they can do for their mental health. Withdrawing from the world and connecting to different levels of consciousness is a way they cope. Dreaming, daydreaming, and sleep are things that Pisces moons value. Taking naps is a way they escape from their problems. Some Pisces moons struggle with insomnia or end up sleeping too much.

Pisces moons are psychic and intuitive and often dream of future events. It is important to keep a dream journal so they can write down messages that come through at night. Investing in a thorough dream interpretation book will help them analyze recurring symbols. Once they understand their dreams, they will realize how their dreams guide their daily life.

Ultimately, Pisces moons want to feel like there is a reason they are on this earth. Naturally spiritual, many believe in a higher power. They value having the freedom to explore spiritual topics. It is important for Pisces moons to study different religions, philosophies, and disciplines in order to find the one that resonates with them the most. Pisces moon people overcome challenging times by connecting to the Universe and finding oneness with a higher power.

Many Pisces moons believe in soul mates. They believe that there are special people in the world they are destined to meet and love. This propels them forward and keeps them hopeful. Romance, love, and intimacy are things Pisces moons value.

PISCES MOON SELF-CARE

Pisces moons need to focus more on their own needs. They sacrifice their time and energy for those who need help, and this cycle never ends because people in pain are attracted to their compassionate nature. Because Pisces moons are natural empaths, other people profoundly affect them in positive and negative ways. The best thing Pisces moon people can do for self-care is develop stronger boundaries. Making extra effort to protect their energy field helps them avoid burnout. One technique that helps is the bubble method. Visualizing a white light surrounding them when they are in large groups of people or when they are in stressful environments will help block out unwanted energy. Another technique can be done in the shower. Pisces moons should visualize dark energy and negative thoughts and feelings washing off their physical body and going down the drain. This is something they can do daily to eliminate negative emotions from their energy field.

Solitude is healing for Pisces moons, and they need to make time to be alone. Escaping from the world in healthy ways allows them to recharge. Calming solo activities include creating art, playing or listening to music, meditating, and spending time in nature, especially near water.

PISCES MOON SELF-CARE PROMPTS

Journaling allows Pisces moons to reflect on their own emotions in solitude. This activity is deeply healing for them.

1. Where do you find passion?

2. What makes you happy?

3. What moon sign traits make you resilient?

4. How can you develop better boundaries?

5. What makes you feel comfortable?

6. How do you handle stress?

7. What is something positive you learned from your mother?

8. What self-care tips are you going to implement?

9. List three things that bring you emotional fulfillment.

10. List three things you are grateful for.

PISCES MOON AFFIRMATIONS

• "I protect myself by developing stronger boundaries."

• "I am connected to a higher power."

• "I take care of myself and my own needs first."

• "I am blessed with artistic and creative talents."

• "I make time for solitary activities."

MOON SIGNS THROUGH THE HOUSES

In this chapter, you can look up the meaning of the moon's placement in each astrological house. The house the moon is placed in reveals where its powerful energy is expressed in the world. Each house represents an area of life, and understanding how the moon reacts in each house can help validate your personal experiences. Wherever the moon is placed in your birth chart is where you express your deepest emotional nature. This chapter provides an in-depth description of how the moon's energy impacts each house—and your life!—so you can learn more about yourself and others.

MOON IN THE FIRST HOUSE

First house moons have a magnetism and high energy that impacts the environment. When you walk into a room, people notice you immediately. Other people perceive first house moons as confident, assertive, brave, charming, and driven.

If the moon is placed in the first house, your emotional nature goes through extremes. There is a tendency to react impulsively, and feelings may become erratic. Emotions can be overwhelming, fierce, and intense. Focused on your own inner life, there are times you ignore the feelings of others. You can get too wrapped up in what you feel and forget about what is happening in others' lives. It makes it difficult to find balance.

With the moon in the first house, reacting to situations with great emotional intensity helps other people know exactly how you feel. People appreciate your honesty, directness, and ability to address conflict head-on. You are known to say what other people don't have the guts to say. You are honest about your feelings and find it hard to hide your emotions; your facial expressions and body language always show how you feel. It's hard for you to be fake or pretend that you are happy—first house moon people are not the best at poker! You'd be better off playing sports where you can compete openly and directly.

Physical appearance, health, and body image are important to first house moons. You put a lot of energy into looking physically fit and value your health. Competition via sports brings comfort and happiness. Winning and being recognized are important when the moon is in the first house. You like a challenge, so the more physical the sport, the better.

There is a powerful emotional force guiding you toward your goals. Just like a ram, you put your horns down and move forward regardless of the obstacles. First house people never give up. Overthinking, planning, and having to wait are all things that irritate first house moons. Listening to your heart and inner voice helps reveal the answers you are seeking. Conquering all obstacles is inevitable because of your powerful emotional force. You are brave and confident, and you fiercely defend what you believe in.

You crave emotional freedom and independence, and you dislike being withheld for any reason. Autonomy is important to you and makes you feel alive. When in love, you are romantic and passionate, and you continuously pursue the object of your desire. First house moons can become consumed by romantic love. Being in love might make you feel off-balance and distract you from your goals. Sometimes you will end relationships abruptly, even when you love someone. You might make decisions you later regret because of your need for immediate results.

The moon represents the mother figure. First house moon people might have experienced their mother as selfish, self-absorbed, assertive, athletic, independent, and passionate. First house moons might feel their mother only focused on her own personal interests, goals, and projects. Sometimes you might have felt neglected or believed that she did not support you fully. At times the mother figure may have been extremely emotional, passive-aggressive, dominant, bossy, and competitive. When the moon is in the first house, you have to learn how to nurture yourself.

You shine whenever you express your inner drives and emotions forcefully and honestly. You will benefit from taking the attention off yourself and putting yourself in other people's shoes. Considering others and not being self-absorbed helps improve your relationships. The moon in the first house is a powerful placement. It blesses you with stamina, strength, and a strong drive to succeed.

MOON IN THE SECOND HOUSE

Craving financial stability first, you feel safest when you can live comfortably in the practical world. There is a desire to own a beautiful home and surround yourself with attractive art and furniture. You may collect antiques or showcase furniture that was given to you by a grandparent. Accumulating material things comes easily, but it might be hard for you to release things even when you know you don't need them anymore. Hoarding can become a problem when the moon is in the second house.

Strong-willed, stubborn, and determined, the moon here makes it hard to let go. Growth comes from releasing what you no longer use. This includes cutting ties with unhealthy family members, romantic partners, and friends. Becoming emotionally bogged down by all the clutter and memories in life can cause stagnation. People from the past will always be a part of your life unless you purposely cut ties. You are emotionally connected to your roots, so you might struggle to forgive and forget. Childhood friends and high school lovers can haunt your memory. Letting go of people can be the most challenging lesson for you to learn.

It is difficult for you to forgive unpleasant feelings and past hurts. The past is very much a part of your present. It's hard for you to release things because your emotions are connected to them; saving old letters, cards, pictures, and movie ticket stubs brings you back to the past, so you resist letting them go. Nostalgia and reminiscing are a big part of your life. Second house moons dislike change, but it's needed to transform unhealthy habits. At times you hold on to things longer than needed, including people who are not supporting your life. Being taken for granted, being used for financial gain, and being part of an unhealthy relationship creates emotional wounds.

The other important lesson that you face is in finding a greater sense of self-worth. Having money and possessions makes life easier, but it will not help you truly love yourself or value your abilities. Material things don't always bring happiness. You sometimes feel that if your outward appearances fall short, then you are not good enough. You might even feel like you don't deserve material security or positive life experiences. Second house moons are special people with a lot to give, regardless of financial status. You deserve to be accepted by others. Thinking about what is actually valuable will begin to impact your life. Your values may change throughout your life and go through several ups and downs. Second house moons are learning to develop self-esteem and self-acceptance. Your primary mission is to balance inner needs with outer needs.

Second house moon people enjoy food, and eating brings great comfort. Be careful about eating too much when stressed or anxious. You don't particularly enjoy exercise, but being more active will help you feel better. Second house moons enjoy being outdoors, gardening, relaxing, entertaining, and listening to music. Pleasure and sensuality are also an important part of life; you are affectionate and enjoy cuddling with those you love. Second house moons need to remember to enjoy life's pleasures in moderation.

The moon represents the mother figure. Second house moons might have experienced the mother figure as strong-willed, stubborn, and possessive, while also being calm, comforting, and supportive. She was traditional, religious, strict, hardworking, and practical. The mother figure taught second house moon people about the importance of money. You may have felt that your mother cared more about possessions than she did about you. Your mother might have been more comfortable buying things for you than she was giving affection. Her thriftiness and stress about financial security could have transferred over to you. You need to be careful not to make financial security and money the focus of your life.

Second house moons can be overly focused on the future and think about retirement at a young age. There is a natural fear of losing possessions. You may worry about never having enough money; with this placement, money brings you emotional security and comfort. As you grow older, you might realize you did not enjoy living life due to deep-seated fears of loss. You may start to use the money you saved to travel, buy a new car, or pursue a hobby that was put on the back burner due to cost. True happiness isn't financial; it is found when you have affection, comfort, self-esteem, and support from those you love. Building a stable foundation and learning to live life with healthy balances will help you reach all your future goals.

MOON IN THE THIRD HOUSE

Third house moons excel at communication and expressing emotions. Without social interaction, you can become depressed and withdrawn. Third house moons like to think and share information with others. Computers, social media, and reaching a wide range of people interests third house moons.

When planets fall in the third house, there is heightened intelligence, an ability to learn quickly, and an increased capability to remember and recall information. Third house moons excel in school due to their photographic memory. If you connect to a subject, then you are more likely to continue studying it.

Being able to challenge your mind by learning new things increases satisfaction. Pursuing intellectually stimulating activities like solving puzzles, reading, writing, playing word games, and teaching others helps conquer boredom. Everything related to early childhood education, such as reading, writing, and basic knowledge, interests third house people. Gifted with strong communication skills and natural teaching abilities, you have a way of making high-level information understandable for the average person. Teaching complex subjects on a basic level is a talent of yours. You find emotional satisfaction in educating others and encouraging people to learn. You are attracted to career fields such as journalism, publishing, and anything involving the radio, media, or television. Expressing what you think is a big part of your sense of emotional stability.

You are talkative, and you have a witty sense of humor. Your sarcasm lightens people's moods. Third house moons are friendly and open-minded. People like you and naturally gravitate toward you because of your easygoing personality. Storytelling comes naturally, and you excel at improvisation because you can shift between personalities at a moment's notice. Socializing and meeting new people is exciting. You enjoy interactions with people at the grocery store, acquaintances, and neighbors. Learning to keep secrets is important, and you need to avoid participating in gossip.

You can have difficulties in relationships due to an inability to keep things private. Third house moons have to learn discretion: there are some things that shouldn't be shared with everyone unless there is trust built. Relationships can end abruptly due to your commitment issues.

Routines create restlessness, and third house moons find happiness by traveling short distances and taking frequent journeys. You enjoy driving in the car, walking around, riding a bike, taking the bus, and commuting to different areas. Contentment will always involve some type of movement.

Sitting still and being cooped up without room to move around can cause disruptions in your mood. Physical activity helps balance your restless mind and emotional nature. Keeping busy and having plenty of hobbies helps calm your nervousness. You are good at working with your hands. Some third house moons excel in endeavors such as carpentry, repairing cars, playing musical instruments, painting, sculpting, or completing household projects.

Third house moons have an abundance of energy that can create problems with resting, relaxing, and sleeping. You often suffer from insomnia and wake up in the middle of the night thinking about things that happened during the day. It is hard to shut your mind off. Creating a stable sleep routine helps; try turning off technology several hours before bed.

Having a close relationship with your siblings is something you need. You tend to create strong bonds with your siblings, and they are an extremely important part of your life. You might have provided nurturing to younger siblings. It's possible you served as a parental figure or took on that role in some way. Third house moons that are only children experience loneliness; you need to have someone to talk to about family issues. If you did not have siblings of your own, friends became like family. Having close friends who feel like siblings can fill the void of not having your own brothers or sisters.

When the moon is in the third house, the mother figure was seen as free-spirited, independent, changeable, restless, and intelligent. She had a lot of hobbies and interests. Education was important to her, and she made sure that intellectual pursuits were prioritized and available throughout your childhood. Your mother figure might have been a social butterfly who enjoyed having friends over to the house. Communicating, gossiping, and discussing different world issues came easily for her. You might have perceived your mother as detached from her emotions, though she was a good communicator and enjoyed talking through problems with the family. Nurturing was found in discussion and communication. You might have learned to doubt your decisions due to overthinking.

Writing and expressing yourself will help balance your restless emotions. Your words are powerful and can change lives.

MOON IN THE FOURTH HOUSE

The moon in the fourth house is one of the most favorable placements. The fourth house is ruled by the moon, so it's in its natural home. Everything that involves your childhood home, current home, and future home can be found here. You are focused on making your home a stable, beautiful, comfortable, and safe place. Emotional security is tied to a solid family environment. If your home is unstable, you will struggle to feel grounded.

Fourth house moons are deeply connected to the past and to family. You are interested in genealogy and family traditions. Thinking about your childhood makes you nostalgic because you had many happy memories. You likely have a strong bond with your parents, especially your mother figure. If that relationship is strained, you can suffer anxiety, guilt, and depression. Your mother was probably nurturing and affectionate. She was a source of encouragement, and you were often spoiled. The home has always been a place where you seek refuge.

If you had a difficult childhood or experienced divorce, separation, or the death of a parent, it had a devastating effect on your ability to trust. If your mother figure was overly emotional, possessive, and depressed, you lacked a solid foundation and often felt lost and disconnected. Fourth house moons need to ensure the home created in adulthood is safe, stable, and supportive. Your happiness will suffer tremendously if there are unstable or toxic people within the home. The home is your sanctuary and a place for you to withdraw; solitude helps you replenish your emotional energy.

Fourth house moon people need time alone to contemplate and process deep emotions. Stress, anxiety, and responsibilities build up and disturb your comfort. You like to escape into your emotional shell to cope with challenges. Just like the waves of the ocean, your emotional nature ebbs and flows, and you experience extreme highs and lows. Your emotions have a strong impact on your life. Learn to be patient with yourself and accept that feelings are changeable.

Fourth house moon people want to take care of others. You often feel others' pain as if it were your own. If someone is suffering or lonely, you will befriend them and listen to their problems. Once you trust someone, you attach to them easily. Friends become like family. Fourth house people are compassionate, sensitive, protective, and dependable. Nurturers at heart, you are fiercely loyal and will do anything for your loved ones. These bonds are difficult to break. Cooking and preparing meals for those you care about makes you happy. Fourth house moons make excellent parents and look forward to having children. Taking care of your children's needs and protecting them comes naturally. You like to cuddle with your children and ensure they feel loved.

Forgiving others can be difficult, especially when your feelings are hurt. You fear being hurt, betrayed, and let down by others. Fourth house moons hold grudges, withdraw, and push people away, especially when feeling insecure. Remember that most people are not like you, and expecting others to take care of you can lead to disappointment. Managing your expectations is key. Spending time with children helps you come out of your hard shell.

When the moon is in the fourth house, the mother figure was seen as nurturing, overprotective, emotional, and kind. She was creative, imaginative, and enjoyed being home. Cooking, cleaning, and taking care of the family were her top priorities. Teaching the importance of family, roots, and heritage was important. Your mother figure might have been a bit controlling and overly involved in your personal life. You have a close bond with your mother figure, even if it's a difficult relationship. She might expect you to take care of her when she grows older, and you might have trouble moving away from her. Living nearby is common with this placement; you may even allow her to live with you.

You are a natural born caregiver, and you attract those who are wounded or emotionally vulnerable. You shine when you can help others in some way.

MOON IN THE FIFTH HOUSE

You enjoy experiencing pleasure and being in love. You are always chasing romance because you want to find someone to connect with. Fifth house moons can be fickle and jump from one love affair to another; dating multiple people brings excitement into your life. Attractions come on strong but fizzle out quickly. Your emotions are changeable, so committing to one person can be challenging. It is important to make sure you have something in common and not just sexual chemistry. There can be emotional ups and downs in your relationships. You are happiest when you have a variety of people to spend time with.

Experiencing pleasure and having fun is your focus. Be cautious about gambling and spending money, because you tend to get involved in risky investments. Be careful not to act on impulsive feelings—you win big sometimes, but you can lose big too. Fifth house moons seek emotional thrills. You like competing and pushing yourself to your limits; challenge makes you feel alive. Expressing your immense amount of physical and creative energy helps balance your emotions.

When the moon is in the fifth house, your emotional nature fluctuates between happiness and depression. You are known to lash out when your feelings are hurt. The best way to snap out of these mood swings is to stay active or express your creativity. You were born with many talents—you are creative and imaginative and an excellent writer and storyteller—but some of your talents won't manifest until you're older. If your creative abilities were not nurtured by your parents during childhood, you will find more confidence in them as you grow.

Being the center of attention and receiving praise brings emotional fulfillment. Joining a group, sports team, or club allows you to show off your talents. You want to feel respected and appreciated at all times. Fifth house moons can feel unloved without constant praise from friends, family, and coworkers. Theater, acting, and singing appeal to you because you enjoy being on stage in front of others; being in the limelight is comfortable. Leading groups or clubs and being an authority figure boosts your mood.

Fifth house moons are children at heart and are incredibly playful. Always looking for a good time is what draws friends into your inner circle. Charming and charismatic, you have the ability to make people laugh, but there is a sweet side to your personality as well. Working with children in some way brings happiness. Many fifth house moon people want to be a parent and have several children. If you don't have children of your own, you might be known as the fun-loving aunt or uncle who wrestles, plays in the mud, and is always first in line to go down the slide. You're a big kid at heart. As a parent, there is nothing you wouldn't do for your children. Supporting and nurturing your children as they find their own self-expression, confidence, and artistic abilities is your priority.

The moon represents the mother figure. You likely experienced your mother figure as energetic, fun-loving, creative, affectionate, confident, and beautiful. Your mother taught you how to express yourself and encouraged you to pursue your creative side. You might have been smothered with affection and spoiled as a child. It's also possible that the mother figure was self-absorbed and focused on her own hobbies.

Be cautious about being so focused on yourself that you accidentally neglect the people in your life. When you acknowledge other people's feelings and support them, you will find true joy.

MOON IN THE SIXTH HOUSE

Sixth house moons are health conscious, practical, organized, and detail focused. Maintaining a sense of order is critical for you to feel secure, and you enjoy having a routine. Structured environments make you feel balanced; chaos, change, and the unknown make you feel uneasy. Sixth house moons are productive and efficient. You are able to work endless hours accomplishing tasks, and most people can't keep up. But overworking and neglecting your own needs can lead to burnout, and stress, worry, and a tendency to overanalyze things can lead to health problems. You need to balance your mind, body, and spirit. Start by implementing breathing exercises into your routine. Recover and recharge by getting away from work at a reasonable hour. Owning a dog or another animal that you can cuddle with is also beneficial.

Sixth house moons might experience unexplained health problems during childhood. Seasonal allergies, food allergies, and unexplained illnesses are often linked to this area of life. Change, instability, and crisis severely affect your health. You have a sensitive body, so obsessive thoughts affect your mood as well. It's important to overcome worry and pessimistic thinking. Focusing on the positive will help you overcome setbacks.

Emotionally high-strung, you may experience stomach problems and digestive issues. You have a strong desire to control your environment and have very high standards. Focus on things you can change and let go of what you have no control over. Being too rigid can impact your work environment. You develop workaholic tendencies because you find contentment in getting things done; checking tasks off your to-do list relieves stress. Reliable and loyal, you believe in responsibility and take your career seriously. If you are not in charge or don't hold a supervisory role, you might feel uneasy and experience anxiety. Moon in the sixth house people are multitaskers and typically work on several projects at once. Very few people can keep up with your high levels of productivity, and problems with coworkers can arise if there is jealousy or competition. You might feel that coworkers and higher-ups don't appreciate your effort or acknowledge how much you accomplish. Peaceful relationships with coworkers are needed in order for you to feel comfortable. Ultimately, you're a team player that wants stability at work.

Perfectionistic tendencies cause you to put additional stress on yourself. No one is perfect. Loving and accepting yourself is a lesson to be learned. Remember that you are human and allowed to make mistakes. If you hyperfixate on negative outcomes, you will stay stuck in a pessimistic cycle of emotions. Sixth house moons benefit from reciting positive affirmations and practicing gratitude. Writing in a gratitude journal encourages you to embrace your weaknesses and transform them.

You crave mental stimulation, and communicating your feelings helps you process unpleasant emotions. Discussing your problems with trusted friends, coworkers, and family members is beneficial.

The moon represents the mother figure. When the moon is placed in the sixth house, you perceived your mother figure as intelligent, health conscious, structured, and organized. You may have felt she was overprotective, obsessive, and too focused on making sure you learned the value of responsibility. She was focused on her career and enjoyed doing things for others; she might have worked in the medical field. As a perfectionist, your mother had high standards for you. She pushed you to succeed in school and set goals for your future. Sometimes you were able to live up to your mother's standards, but when you didn't, it affected your self-esteem. Sixth house moons can suffer from a fear of failure and experience anxiety about messing things up.

When the moon is in the sixth house, there is often a love of small animals. Your pets become your children, and you are very attached to them. Working with animals, adopting abused or neglected pets, or finding a career where you can work with animals in some way brings fulfillment. Sixth house moons are drawn to professions that serve others in some way. Helping make people's lives better is your mission. You might pursue work in the fields of healthcare, social work, psychology, childcare, veterinary medicine, or education.

MOON IN THE SEVENTH HOUSE

Seventh house moons are calm, peaceful, intellectual, and artistic. You are a peacemaker at heart and dislike conflict; much of your identity morphs to please others. Seventh house moons are emotional chameleons. You can adapt and get along with anyone. Charming, flirtatious, and attractive, it's hard for others not to like you. You know what to say to make others laugh and can be the life of the party.

Your emotional security comes from having a significant other and being in love. Being alone does not suit you—you feel best when attached to someone. Make sure that your desire for an emotional connection does not push you into the arms of a toxic partner. You need a reliable, stable, and supportive partner who will take care of you. Benefits can come through your partner, so it's important to choose wisely. If you get involved in dysfunctional relationships, it will destroy your happiness and emotional stability. You tend to sacrifice your own happiness for your partner, but it is important not to neglect yourself. Don't be afraid of expressing your own needs. Taking care of your partner can be emotionally rewarding, but there should be reciprocity in all of your relationships.

Moon in the seventh house people experience mood swings. When your personal relationships are solid, you snap out of negative emotions faster. Sadness, depression, and anxiety pop up out of the blue, then quickly shift to happiness, contentment, and positivity. Like a yo-yo, your emotional nature goes up and down. Having support from your family and friends during difficult times is especially useful for you. Loved ones might be confused by your emotional changes—communication is the key. Working out problems and conflict helps you realize that disagreements are a normal part of life. Resist the urge to be passive; standing up for yourself is critical in order to get your needs met. Taking charge of your emotional life and making your own decisions will help you grow stronger as a person. Marriage and business partnerships often go through ups and downs with the moon placed here.

When the moon is in the seventh house, your mother figure was seen as beautiful and pleasant. Artistic, talented, and creative, your mother might have passed these gifts on to you or your siblings. Your mother's mood might have been confusing; she might have experienced periods of depression, loneliness, and sadness. The mother figure might have been self-absorbed and focused on her own life. Your relationship with your mother figure taught you a lot about compromise. She also taught you about commitment and relationships, and this had profound positive or negative effects on you. If your parents divorced or if you were raised by a single parent, this will influence your beliefs about love. Intimate relationships are impacted by your mother's influence. Be cautious about valuing your mother's opinions more than anyone else's; partnerships might struggle because of the relationship you have with her.

There might be times you are single and experience indecision about commitment. These periods of singleness are the perfect time for you to work on yourself. Learn to speak up for yourself and share your opinions freely.

MOON IN THE EIGHTH HOUSE

Eighth house moons are born with intuitive and psychic abilities. Unexplained experiences are common. Highly emotional and perceptive, you need to listen to your inner voice. You are drawn to the mysteries of life and from a young age you were interested in the soul, death, spirits, and dreams. Your life was impacted by death at a young age. Loss of a parent, friend, or close family member transformed your life and changed how you see the world. Your experience with grief helps you find a spiritual path.

Being afraid of the dark is common for eighth house moons. You may sense there are people in your room, and your imagination can run wild. Your mind is focused on things that are taboo, scary, and difficult for most people to talk about. Eighth house moon people are afraid of dying or losing a loved one. Questions pop into your mind like *What if I die? Where will I go?* Some eighth house moons are not afraid of death at all and have indescribable experiences with spirits, ghosts, and deceased loved ones. You might have mediumship abilities and be able to connect to the other side.

Intense and secretive, eighth house moons are strong and resilient. Your emotional nature goes through extreme highs and lows. You hide what you feel because you don't think others will understand. You feel different from others; sometimes it's like you are on the outside looking in. Because you are secretive, those closest to you sometimes have no idea when you are struggling. Feeling lonely even among family and friends is common.

Eighth house moons are wounded healers: you transform your own wounds when you alleviate the pain of others. People who have experienced traumatic experiences are drawn to you for healing. Your energy draws individuals into your life that need help. Nothing shocks or surprises you; you are able to listen and give advice on a variety of issues. Remember not to take on the problems of others—you are not responsible for their burdens. Your ability to heal others can cause difficulties if you do not develop stronger boundaries to protect your own energy. Be careful not to drain yourself of energy or take on other people's pain as your own.

Your energy vibrates at a high level and you absorb everyone's thoughts, feelings, and emotions. Repressed emotions can cause illness, so it's important to express them in healthy ways. Exercise, meditation, and relaxation techniques can be helpful.

You have an ability to sense the motivations, subconscious thoughts, and emotions of others. Secret, taboo, and hidden things stand out to you; you notice them instantly. You need to trust your perceptions and use these abilities to help others. You pull out people's secrets, so just by being in your presence, others can feel vulnerable. Sometimes you feel like others are trying to hurt you purposely. Eighth house moons struggle with anger, anxiety, and depression. Accept the fact that you are special and your energy vibrates higher than others. Some people feel comfortable with that, and others will run away. Controlling your insecurities and gaining control of your psychic abilities helps you feel more in control.

Eighth house moon people feel victimized by others. There is often a wound surrounding issues with trust, vulnerability, and intimacy. Passionate, intense, and deep, you want to bond with another person on all levels. When you have sexual intercourse with someone, you merge with that person on a spiritual level. It can be difficult for you not to experience jealousy, insecurity, possessiveness, and controlling behaviors. You want a commitment and expect total loyalty from others.

Suffering often comes at the hands of people you love. Sometimes you feel people have used you for sex or for their own benefit. This trauma brings up issues from childhood and abuse that you have not healed from. Eighth house moons are survivors. You will be transformed, reborn, and regenerated throughout life. Like the phoenix, you rise from the ashes and transform into a wiser, stronger, and more resilient person.

Eighth house moons are drawn to healing careers. Bringing the unconscious into conscious awareness interests you. Psychiatry, psychology, medicine, hypnotherapy, energy healing, and spiritual work are areas where you shine. Diving deep into life issues and helping other people process grief, loss, and tragedy is a natural gift. Insightful and compassionate, you are a supportive ally for anyone who is struggling. Eighth house moons are excellent listeners. Sending healing energy to others helps you connect; you might want to study Reiki energy healing, pranic healing, or healing touch modalities. You are able to understand others' pain because you know what it's like to lose someone.

When the moon is in the eighth house, your mother figure was seen as mysterious, deep, brooding, mystical, and controlling. You may have perceived her as private, distant, and secretive. She might have experienced bouts of intense anger, grand emotional displays, or periods of being very withdrawn. She taught you how to keep secrets and instilled in you the importance of trusting others. Your mother figure might have been psychic and passionate about metaphysical topics like astrology, tarot, and healing. Emotional nurturing might have been lacking due to her inability to share her own feelings, but you saw her as powerful, strong, and independent. Eighth house moons may have lost their mother figure at a young age through sudden death or illness. You will inherit something (land, property, possessions, money, or psychic abilities) from your mother or from someone on her side of the family. Financial success and material items will almost always come to you from someone else, such as a family member, partner, or parent.

The moon in the eighth house is a blessing and a curse: the blessing is that you will be a true healer and able to serve others in a deep way; the curse is that you are often lonely in relationships and feel that no one relates to you. Realize that your feelings of loneliness will cease once you see your oneness with others instead of your separateness.

MOON IN THE NINTH HOUSE

Ninth house moons find happiness in traveling, knowledge, and spirituality. You were born with a natural belief in God and have a strong faith that is almost unshakable. You may enjoy studying religion and philosophy.

Ninth house moons' emotional nature is restless and needs frequent movement; you dislike being cooped up. Traveling, exploring, and adventure make you feel alive. You befriend people from different religions, ethnicities, and cultures. Surrounding yourself with people who are different and who can teach you new things is exciting. Learning about other countries and cultures expands your mind. Ninth house moons often live in a foreign country at some point in life. You might have been a military brat and moved a lot in childhood or joined the military yourself. If you did not travel or move around during childhood, that will be a big part of your life when you are older. Exploring exotic, faraway places inspires your sense of adventure.

Ninth house moons need diversity in life and enjoy trying different foods, attending religious services, and listening to others' beliefs. Rebelling against the religion your parents taught you can cause guilt, but you may feel that a different religion suits you better. You fight strongly for the things you believe in, and having freedom to be yourself is important to you. Born with a courageous spirit, you have a talent for motivating others to believe in themselves.

In relationships, ninth house moons need to feel free. You are attracted to people who are different from you in some way. You are naturally happy, outgoing, and carefree, so having fun with your partner is key. You dislike feeling tied down to anyone. Restless at heart, you may struggle with commitment. You are an adventurous partner who likes to explore the world with your loved ones.

You are likely attracted to career fields where you can expand your mind, learn things, teach others, and master a skill. You need movement, travel, and variety in your career. You may join the military so you can travel the world and live in different countries. Ninth house moons tend to marry someone from another country or culture.

When the moon is in the ninth house, your mother figure was seen as adventurous, intelligent, free-spirited, and friendly. You may have perceived her as restless because she was always on the move. She may be from a different culture or religious background; she may have been bilingual. Your parents might have met when traveling, or your mother might have grown up in a foreign country. You learn a lot about the world from your mother. She raised you to be understanding of different religions, cultures, and beliefs. You learned a lot about spirituality from her. Open-minded, she taught you to think broadly and educate yourself. She might have encouraged you to pursue higher education, obtained advanced degrees, or been a professor.

Optimistic, happy, and generous, you are always wandering and seeking new experiences. Ninth house moons need time to explore and visit never-before-seen places. Not being able to travel causes depression, restlessness, frustration, and anxiety. You like to feel the wind in your hair and have fun. Attending concerts, driving around in a convertible, bungee jumping, hiking outdoors, and anything that boosts adrenaline helps you feel free.

MOON IN THE TENTH HOUSE

Your sense of self is strongest when you feel financially and materially secure. Having a large salary and owning expensive things raises your self-esteem. Your family had high expectations of you from a young age, and if you do not feel that you are making enough money, you can become depressed, angry, and irritable. Your family is full of high achievers.

Being recognized for your work ethic makes you feel valued. You need to feel in control of things in your work environment. Organization, structure, and routine are important. If you are not a supervisor or in a leadership role, you will always be seeking more responsibility. Obtaining a leadership position where you can inspire large groups of people brings contentment. Tenth house moons work well in politics.

Tenth house moons are focused on moving up the career ladder. When the moon is in the tenth house, women can be a beneficial influence in your career and open doors for you. Marrying someone more successful than you is common. Because you are so focused on your own career, you might put off marriage or marry later in life. Be careful not to push away healthy love interests because of your desire to achieve a high status. Later in your life, you may regret giving up certain opportunities; you may have success but go home each night to an empty house.

Developing a work-life balance is beneficial for your overall happiness. Learning how to let go of your sense of responsibility helps you live life to the fullest. You need to make time for fun. Going on vacation, enjoying your favorite hobbies, and hanging out with family helps you relax. You need to make sure to nurture the relationships with your loved ones.

When the moon is in the tenth house, the mother figure was practical, hardworking, controlling, and reliable. She encouraged you to work hard and be responsible; status and recognition were important to her. She wanted the best for you and taught you the value of success. Your mother had a way of making friends with the right people, and they were often influential. Your mother figure had a lucrative career and worked very hard to achieve her goals. Making money was important to her, and she encouraged you to enter career fields that pay well. You might have viewed your mother as emotionally distant, cold, and aloof; you may feel that she neglected her own family to pursue her goals. You may have unhealed issues regarding your mother and her lack of nurturing or support. It is likely that your mother was dominant and played the father figure role in your life as well.

Tenth house moons are guided by achievement and obtaining positions of authority. You crave a solid career, recognition, and fame—deep down, there is a desire to be in the limelight. Your stamina is focused on work and being productive. If things are not going well at work, you become stressed and can take your feelings out on your loved ones. Cultivating healthy relationships should be a priority.

MOON IN THE ELEVENTH HOUSE

Eleventh house moons value friendship. They have a happy-go-lucky quality and a natural ability to make people feel better. Being a part of a group or club helps you feel accepted. Spending time with friends socializing, learning, and collaborating on projects makes you happy. Doing things that help large groups of people gives you a sense of purpose. Humanitarians at heart, eleventh house moons are great at organizing social events. This is a positive place for the moon. Nonjudgmental and open-minded, you expect others to treat everyone equally. Networking is your talent, and you are able to bring people together to work on a common goal.

You easily help people with their problems; you like to alleviate other people's suffering. It's hard for you to be happy if you witness others struggling. You care about economic fairness, equal rights, and solving the world's problems. Because you are emotionally detached, you have a realistic way of giving advice to others without taking on their problems. Some people might judge eleventh house moons harshly. You may be accused of being cold, aloof, or not interested in what others feel. That isn't true—you just have a very cerebral approach to emotion. When you have a strong feeling, your immediate response is to question and analyze it. You are fascinated by how people think and what they believe. You prefer having relationships with people who share similar values and beliefs. You like to spend time with friends discussing real-world problems.

If you aren't able to spend quality time with your friends, you may feel lonely. You have many acquaintances because of your easygoing personality. Friendly, talkative, and intelligent, helping others connect over a shared mission brings comfort. While others in your life enjoy being alone, you prefer to spend time surrounded by other people, and you tend to rely heavily on friends and partners for your happiness.

Committing in relationships is challenging because you are a free spirit. Many people with the moon in the eleventh house choose not to marry and prefer to date. In order to fall in love, you need to develop a social connection and be friends first. Friends become lovers with this placement. Communication is important to you, as is having someone who respects your need for autonomy. If a partner is clingy, you will rebel and quickly move on.

Imaginative, you like to daydream and fantasize about the future. You spend a lot of time in your own head thinking about societal rules and how to make the world a better place. Your hopes, wishes, and dreams often go through many changes, as do your friendships. Eleventh house moons may become friends with emotionally unstable people and individuals that are unique, eccentric, or creative. Expressing your wildest dreams with others helps you feel supported. You might prefer to have a mental connection over an emotional connection, which could lead to several platonic relationships.

Eleventh house moons might join the peace corps, work to solve homelessness, or fight for the rights of children. Solving social problems is where you spend most of your emotional energy. You are able to open up other people's minds with your belief in fairness, equality, and diversity.

You like to shock people by being unique and different. You're normally attracted to people that are very different from you, and you are easily bored with traditional relationships. You might not desire having biological children but instead have an interest in adopting or becoming a foster parent.

When the moon is in the eleventh house, your mother figure was very active in the community, either in groups or politics. She might have been intellectual, independent, and distant. Activities with your mother were often intellectual, and she encouraged your love of knowledge and reading. She was not comfortable giving physical affection, so you might have lacked nurturing and affection in childhood. Your mother figure may have believed feelings were illogical and taught you to analyze them before making important decisions. You learned from your mother to doubt and question your emotions.

Being part of a movement that is making transformative change is the source of your inspiration. Your happiness depends on the social circles you belong to and the impact you have on people in need.

MOON IN THE TWELFTH HOUSE

Twelfth house moons are compassionate, intuitive, and spiritual. Following a spiritual path and believing in a higher power gives you strength. You were born with psychic abilities, but you tend to doubt your own intuition and impressions. Your spiritual gifts are deep and transformative, and you must embrace them. Automatic writing, journaling, and recording your dreams can be helpful tools for self-awareness. Escaping from the stress and responsibilities of the world is common. Using alcohol or other substances to numb your emotions can lead to addictive behaviors. Try to find healthy outlets to handle stress, anxiety, and feelings of depression.

Sometimes you feel like you are living in a dream or fog, making it difficult to see clearly or communicate your true feelings. As a natural empath, you absorb the thoughts and feelings of others in your environment. You even feel other people's pain, to the point that you sometimes don't know whether the pain you are feeling is yours or someone else's. Twelfth house moons are service oriented and want to help people who are suffering. You must be careful, though, because you lack boundaries and tend to attract people that have problems. Twelfth house moons are drawn to psychology, social work, counseling, astrology, and healing. Your giving nature and kindness are often taken for granted.

Kind and sensitive, you sacrifice your own needs for others, but withdrawing from the world will help you recover your energy. Music is an important tool that brings you comfort in times of stress; listening to soothing music helps you connect with your emotions. Twelfth house moons are artistic and many are musicians, actors, or talented artists.

Underneath your friendly and social demeanor, you are an extremely sensitive and shy person. You often hide your true feelings because you don't think people will understand them. Feeling isolated and different from others is common. Sometimes you feel like an alien or like you are very different from your family.

You are highly intuitive and just know things about people and situations. You might struggle with anxiety, depression, or loneliness. You benefit from writing about your emotions or talking about them with someone you trust. Don't be afraid to seek counseling or medication if that will help balance your mood. You tend to be hard on yourself.

Feeling drained emotionally, mentally, and physically happens when you are in groups of people. You attract people who have problems, so you may be drawn to working as a counselor or healer. You do better one-on-one or when you can enjoy solitary activities. Self-care techniques are critical for twelfth house moons. Meditation, breathing exercises, stretching, yoga, and energy healing can help you relax. Spending time alone recharges your social battery.

When the moon is in the twelfth house, your mother figure was sensitive, creative, and compassionate. She may have been very spiritual and blessed you with psychic abilities and knowledge; she was your spiritual role model. The relationship you had with your mother was complex and emotionally burdensome; you felt responsible for her happiness and mental health. Your mother may have suffered from depression, addiction, or loneliness. You perceived her as emotionally vulnerable and unstable and felt you had to be strong for her. You may have felt like you were the parent and your mother was the child, or you may have felt like your mother's older sibling. If you had to take care of your mother figure emotionally, physically, or financially, you might not have had your own emotional needs met. You grew up quickly and had to learn to nurture yourself. You likely have an emotional wound related to your mother. Even though there were struggles in your relationship with your mother figure, you had an unshakeable bond with her and felt extremely loyal to her.

You genuinely care about helping people and work hard to make other people's lives better. Take time to replenish your energy so you can go back out in the world again and serve—you can't help others if your energy is depleted. Learn to put your own needs first and don't sacrifice your own happiness for others.

CONCLUSION

U nderstanding your moon sign and its house placement gives you a deeper understanding of who you really are. I learned more about my strengths when I tapped into the energy of my Aries moon sign. I was able to embrace a deeper part of my emotional nature and learned how to control my impatience, temper, strong reactions, and need for independence. Utilizing my sun sign *and* moon sign traits created a great balance. I feel my moon sign's energy has helped me overcome challenges and encouraged me to heal through sheer determination. At times, I feel more like my moon sign than my sun sign.

Learning more about your moon sign helps you get in touch with deeper emotions. Once you know how to tap into your emotional strengths, you can heal, transform, and become more resilient. When you learn to express feelings in healthy ways, you find greater balance in all areas of your life. With hard work and patience, you will be able to balance mind, body, and spirit. Your moon sign's gifts are always there waiting for you—the key is to keep learning about them.

TO WRITE TO THE AUTHOR

If you wish to contact the author or would like more information about this book, please write to the author in care of Llewellyn Worldwide Ltd. and we will forward your request. Both the author and publisher appreciate hearing from you and learning of your enjoyment of this book and how it has helped you. Llewellyn Worldwide Ltd. cannot guarantee that every letter written to the author can be answered, but all will be forwarded. Please write to:

Carmen Turner-Schott
⁒ Llewellyn Worldwide
2143 Wooddale Drive
Woodbury, MN 55125-2989
Please enclose a self-addressed stamped envelope for reply,
or $1.00 to cover costs. If outside the U.S.A., enclose
an international postal reply coupon.

Many of Llewellyn's authors have websites with additional information and resources. For more information, please visit our website at http://www.llewellyn.com.